The Ultimate Shooter Drink Directory

Includes Recipes for 1600 New & Classic Shooters

Dennis A. Wildberger

The Ultimate Shooter Drink Directory

The only shooter guide you will ever need!

Includes 1600 New & Classic Shooter Recipes

Written and Compiled by:

Dennis A. Wildberger

Introduction

Mixing drinks is both an art and a science. The art is easy: create a pleasant-tasting, attractive-looking cocktail in a clean glass with the proper garnish. The science is harder.

The science of cocktail making involves many things. It is knowing the exact ingredients for the drink you are building. Knowing the exact measurements of the aforementioned ingredients. Knowing which glass is the proper glass for each specific drink. Knowing how much ice to use. "Up" or "on the rocks". What is the proper garnish? Etcetera, etcetera.

It is impossible for one human being to physically remember the details of every drink recipe ever created. Who would want to? It is for that reason, in part, that I created the "Ultimate Shooter Drink Directory".

Now, I'm not claiming that within these pages you will find the recipe for every shooter drink ever invented. However, what you will find here are the recipes for the most popular, classic, and creative shooters ever consumed.

Many of the recipes in this book come from twenty years of personal experience working behind the bars of countless pubs, cafes, nightclubs, and restaurants. Very early on, I became a student of the bar industry. I strove to learn everything I could about the craft of bartending. I wanted to learn how to make every cocktail imaginable. I bought the few drink books that were available, studied them, and was disappointed every time. Not only was each bartender's guide short on recipes, they were all just duplicates of each other, and for the most part, out-of-date.

I decided that if I wanted to learn the recipes, I had to go to the source: my customers and my fellow bartenders. If someone requested a drink that I didn't know how to make, I was not shy about asking (in a way that didn't make me look like an idiot) "do you know what's in that?" Many a night I came home from the job with a pocketful of recipes that I had hurriedly scribbled on cocktail napkins as the patron rattled off the ingredients for a drink I'd never heard of.

Most of these recipes come courtesy of bartenders from all corners of the world. Some of these drinks are house specialties, some of these are bartender specialties. Most of these are just good drinks. One thing is for sure in any case: I thank each and every one of you who took the time to write down the ingredients for all of those thousands and thousands of creative (and tasty) cocktails you've given, sent, or emailed me over the years. Without you, the bartending profession would not be the same.

Within these pages, you will find the proper recipes for all of the classic shooters. More importantly, you will find them in alphabetical order. If you know the name, just look it up!

I have done my best to stay true to the exact ingredients in each recipe. If the original drink (as it was relayed to me) called for, let's say, Midori Melon Liqueur, the recipe, as it is written in this book, reads that way. However, it is up to you, the mixologist, to decide for yourself whether you will use any substitutions.

Enjoy!

Making the Perfect Shooter

Shooters, for all intents and purposes, are simply a combination of ingredients, shaken or stirred with ice, and strained into a particular glass. Here are the procedures broken down into steps:

Stirred & Strained Shooters
1. Choose the proper glass (shooter, large shot, etc.).
2. With an ice scoop, fill a mixing glass half way with ice.
3. Add liquid ingredients to the mixing glass, one ingredient at a time.
4. With a long-handled bar spoon, stir cocktail one time.
5. Place cocktail strainer on top of the mixing glass.
6. Holding strainer and mixing glass firmly, strain cocktail into glass.
7. Add proper garnish, as required.

Shaken & Strained Shooters
1. Choose the proper glass (shooter, large shot, etc.).
2. With an ice scoop, fill mixing glass half way with ice.
3. Add liquid ingredients to the mixing glass, one ingredient at a time.
4. Cover mixing glass with a shaker tin.
5. Shake cocktail approximately 3 times.
6. Leaving cocktail in the shaker tin, remove mixing glass.
7. Place cocktail strainer on top of the shaker tin.
8. Holding strainer and shaker tin firmly, strain cocktail into glass.
9. Add proper garnish, as required.

Layered Shooters
1. Place proper glass on a steady, level surface.
2. According to recipe instructions, pour the first ingredient into the glass.
3. Hold a bar spoon, bowl-side down, against the inside of the glass so that the tip of the spoon is just touching the top of the previous ingredient.
4. Slowly pour next ingredient in recipe over the back of the spoon so that it sits on previous ingredient.
5. Repeat steps 3 and 4, as necessary.

Rimming a Glass

Several recipes in this book require a rimmed glass. Rimming is simply moistening the rim of a glass with a liquid, and dipping the rim into sugar, salt or other condiment. It is easy to accomplish, and can be done very quickly. Commercial glass rimmers (See "Rimmers" in the Bar Supplies section) do make the job easier, but are not necessary. If you don't have a glass rimmer, pour your salt, sugar, or condiment onto a paper or ceramic plate that is wide enough to accommodate the rim of the glass. Here are the steps to take to rim a glass:

1. Choose the proper glass for the shooter you are making.
2. Using a fruit wedge or slice, moisten the rim of the glass by running the pulp of the fruit around the edge of the glass.
3. Gently dip the rim of the glass into the sugar, salt, or spice (as required).
4. Set the glass upright, and allow the rim to dry for a few seconds.

Typical Glassware Used For Shooters:

Shot Glass - (1 - 1 1/2 oz.) - for single liquor shots and small shooters as called for.

Large Shot Glass - (1 1/2 - 2 oz.) - for double shots and shooters as called for.

Lowball or Shooter - (4 - 6 oz.) - for single or double liquors and most shooters.

Accessories You Will Need To Make The Perfect Shooter:

To create the perfect shooter, it is important that you have at your disposal certain items to make the job easier. Here is a list of some of the crucial accessories you should have:

Shaker Tins - Shaker tins are used for exactly what the name implies: to shake drinks when required. They are available in a host of sizes, are commonly made of easy- to-clean polished stainless steel, and last a long, long time. It is recommended that you always have two different-sized tins on hand. A large shaker, usually 16 to 18 ounces, and a smaller 12-ounce tin.

Mixing Glass - A clear mixing glass is an invaluable bar accessory. Used for shaking or stirring cocktails, it allows you to visibly see the drink ingredients as they are added. A 16-ounce pint glass works well. When the large shaker tin is used as a cover or cap for the mixing glass, you have created the perfect cocktail shaker set.

Cocktail Strainer - A cocktail strainer is absolutely necessary. Made of stainless steel with a large curled spring-like coil attached to it, a strainer will allow you to make those "up" drinks very easily. When placed on top of a shaker tin or mixing glass, it holds back the ice cubes in the cocktail for straining.

Ice Scoop - A small ice scoop in your ice bin is absolutely required to help you to quickly fill your glasses or shakers with the necessary amount of ice cubes. (Never use a cocktail glass to scoop ice. If that glass breaks, you certainly will have a mess.)

Bar Spoon - A long-handled, stainless steel spoon will allow you to easily stir the cocktails you have created.

Can Opener - Also know as a "church key", this item is needed for opening juice cans and such.

Blender - A good-quality blender is essential for making those delicious frozen drinks. Normally, the blender cup will hold up to 64 ounces, so you can make double or triple batches at the same time. I prefer a heavy-duty blender with a stainless steel cup that has a tight-fitting plastic or rubber lid.

Jigger Measure - A jigger measure is a convenient way to accurately measure the exact ingredients in your cocktails. Made of stainless steel or plastic, one side of a normal jigger holds 1/2 ounce, the other side holds one full ounce.

Speed Pourers - All of your frequently used liquor bottles should be topped with a speed pourer. They allow you to accurately create a precise stream of liquid without going through the hassle of removing the cap from the bottle. Speed pourers should fit snuggly into the bottle.

Measured Pourer - Similar to the speed pourer, a measured pourer will allow only a certain amount of fluid to pass through it before it automatically cuts off. These are good as a timesaving method, and for helping you measure exact amounts, but can occasionally be irritating. Measured pourers are commonly available in one ounce and 1 1/4 ounce pours.

Funnel - A small funnel should always be kept behind your bar. It is a invaluable tool in transferring liquids from one container to another without spillage.

Glass Rimmer - A nice accessory to have. It will allow you to quickly "rim" your cocktail glass with salt or another condiment for margaritas or other drinks, as necessary. Professional glass rimmers commonly have three separate compartments: one to hold salt, one to hold sugar, and the other that has a round sponge insert that can be moistened with fruit juice. They fold up nicely for storage.

Storage Bottles - Also known as "store-&-pour" containers, these plastic bottles are excellent for refrigerating juices. Since it is not advised to store juices in the can after they are opened (the can will impart a "tinny" flavor), transferring the juice to a storage bottle is recommended. They have a speed pour-type top, are color-coded to match the juice (red for tomato, etc.), and are dishwasher safe.

Condiment Tray - A necessary and convenient item to have to hold all of your pre-cut garnishes, olives, etc. Most condiment trays have removable, individual compartments and a hinged lid. They are available in plastic or stainless steel.

Storage Jars - These are great to have available for refrigerating excess garnishes, fruit, etc. Made of plastic with a tight-fitting screw-top lid, most are dishwasher safe.

1 1 0%
¾ oz. Southern Comfort
¾ oz. Amaretto
¾ oz. Drambuie

Shake all ingredients with ice
and strain into a shooter glass.

100 Octane Gasoline
1 oz. 100 Proof Vodka
½ oz. Wilderberry Schnapps
¼ oz. Cherry Vodka
1 oz. Sour Mix

Shake all ingredients with ice
and strain into a shooter glass.

101 Degrees in the Shade
1 oz. Draft Beer
1 oz. Absolut Peppar Vodka
1 oz. Tomato Juice
2 Dashes Tabasco Sauce

Combine all ingredients in a
shooter glass.

1812 Overture
1 oz. Chambord
1 oz. Vodka

Chill ingredients separately,
then layer in a shooter glass.

1-900-FUK-MEUP
¼ oz. Absolut Kurant Vodka
¼ oz. Grand Marnier
¼ oz. Chambord
¼ oz. Melon Liqueur
¼ oz. Malibu Rum
¼ oz. Amaretto
¼ oz. Cranberry Juice
¼ oz. Pineapple Juice

Shake all ingredients with ice
and strain into a shooter glass.

2 5 2
1 oz. Bacardi 151 Rum
1 oz. Wild Turkey 101

Combine both ingredients in a
shooter glass.

24-Carat Nightmare
1 oz. Goldschlager
1 oz. Tequila
1 oz. Cola

Combine all ingredients in a
shooter glass.

3 Sheets to the Wind
¾ oz. Bacardi 151 Rum
¾ oz. Rumple Minze
¾ oz. Jägermeister

Shake all ingredients with ice
and strain into a shooter glass.

52nd Avenue
1 oz. Pear Liqueur
1 oz. Baileys Irish Cream
1 oz. Creme de Banana

Shake all ingredients with ice
and strain into a shooter glass.

57 Chevy
½ oz. Southern Comfort
½ oz. Amaretto
1 ½ oz. Blue Curacao

Shake all ingredients with ice
and strain into a shooter glass.

57 T-Bird with Florida Plates
¾ oz. Vodka
¾ oz. Amaretto
¾ oz. Grand Marnier
¾ oz. Orange Juice

Shake all ingredients with ice
and strain into a shooter glass.

69er
1 oz. Creme de Banana
1 oz. Light Creme de Cacao
1 oz. Baileys Irish Cream

Shake all ingredients with ice
and strain into a shooter glass.

7 2 7
¾ oz. Rum Cream Liqueur
¾ oz. Amaretto
¾ oz. Kahlua

Shake all ingredients with ice
and strain into a shooter glass.

7 4 7
1 ½ oz. Vodka
1 ½ oz. Licor 43
1 oz. Pineapple Juice

Shake all ingredients with ice
and strain into a shooter glass.

8 Seconds
¾ oz. Hot Damn Cinnamon
Schnapps
¾ oz. Goldschlager
¾ oz. Bacardi 151 Rum

Shake all ingredients with ice
and strain into a shooter glass.

9 1 1 Emergency
1 oz. Cinnamon Schnapps
1 oz. Peppermint Schnapps

Shake both ingredients with ice and strain into a shooter glass.

94th's All-American Treat
1 ½ oz. Applejack
¾ oz. Cinnamon Schnapps

Combine both ingredients in a shooter glass. Top with whipped cream and a cherry.

9mm
¾ oz. Tequila
¾ oz. Hot Damn Cinnamon Schnapps

Combine both ingredients in a shooter glass.

A Gang Bang
Dash of Amaretto
Dash of Galliano
Dash of Apple Schnapps
Dash of Noyeaux
Dash of Grenadine
Dash of Bourbon
Dash of Anisette
Dash of Nutmeg
Dash of Green Chartreuse

Shake all ingredients with ice and strain into a shooter glass.

A. J. B.
1 oz. Amaretto
1 oz. Jägermeister
1 oz. Baileys Irish Cream

Shake all ingredients with ice and strain into a shooter glass.

A.S.S.
1/3 oz. Absolut Vodka
1/3 oz. Spearmint Schnapps
1/3 oz. Sambuca (White)

Combine all ingredients in a shot glass.

Aardvark
1 oz. Parfait Amour
1 oz. Tia Maria
1 oz. Cream

Shake all ingredients with ice and strain into a shooter glass.

Abilene Iced Tea
1 oz. Vodka
½ oz. Lemonade
½ oz. Dr. Pepper
Dash of Grenadine

Shake all ingredients with ice and strain into a shooter glass.

Abortion
¾ oz. Dark Creme de Cacao
¾ oz. Baileys Irish Cream

Layer ingredients in order given in a shooter glass. Top with a few drops of Grenadine.

Absolut Disaster
1 ½ oz. Absolut Vodka
1 ½ oz. Rumple Minze

Shake both ingredients with ice and strain into a shooter glass.

Absolut Fuck
1 oz. Absolut Vodka
¼ oz. Wilderberry Schnapps
½ oz. Grape Pucker Schnapps
½ oz. Cherry Pucker Schnapps
1 oz. Pineapple Juice

Shake all ingredients with ice and strain into a shooter glass.

Absolut Hunter
1 ½ oz. Absolut Vodka
1 ½ oz. Jägermeister

Stir both ingredients with ice and strain into a shooter glass.

Absolut Royal Fuck
½ oz. Absolut Kurant Vodka
1 oz. Crown Royal
½ oz. Peach Schnapps
Splash of Cranberry Juice
Splash of Pineapple Juice

Shake all ingredients with ice and strain into a shooter glass.

Absolut Sizzle
1 ½ oz. Absolut Peppar Vodka
½ oz. Anisette
Splash of Cola

Stir all ingredients with ice and strain into a shooter glass.

Absolut Ultimate Shooter
1 oz. Absolut Peppar Vodka
¼ oz. Cocktail Sauce
¼ oz. Horseradish Sauce

Stir together all ingredients in a shooter glass. Top with a squeeze of fresh lemon juice.

Absolutly Hot
1 oz. Absolut Peppar Vodka
Dash of Tabasco Sauce

Combine both ingredients in a
shot glass. Serve with a beer
chaser.

Acid Cookie
¼ oz. Rumple Minze
¼ oz. Baileys Irish Cream
¼ oz. Butterscotch Schnapps
½ oz. Bacardi 151 Rum
1 oz. Cream

Shake all ingredients with ice
and strain into a shooter glass.

Acid Kick
1 ½ oz. Grain Alcohol
3 Dashes Tabasco Sauce
Squeeze of Fresh Lemon Juice

Combine all ingredients in a
shooter glass.

Acid Trip
1 ½ oz. Melon Liqueur
½ oz. Gin
½ oz. Vodka
½ oz. Rum
½ oz. Tequila

Shake all ingredients with ice
and strain into a shooter glass.

Acidic Eyeball
½ oz. Vodka
½ oz. Blackberry Brandy
½ oz. Triple Sec

Shake all ingredients with ice
and strain into a shooter glass.
Drop a white grape into the
drink.

Adios Mother Fucker
1 oz. Kahlua
1 oz. Tequila

Layer ingredients in order
given in a shooter glass.

Affair
1 oz. Strawberry Schnapps
1 oz. Cranberry Juice
1 oz. Orange Juice

Shake all ingredients with ice
and strain into a shooter glass.

After 8
1 oz. Kahlua
1 oz. Green Creme de Menthe
1 oz. Baileys Irish Cream

Shake all ingredients with ice
and strain into a shooter glass.

After 8 Mint
1 oz. Tia Maria
1 oz. Peppermint Schnapps
1 oz. Kahlua

Shake all ingredients with ice
and strain into a shooter glass.

After Five
1 oz. Kahlua
1 oz. Peppermint Schnapps
1 oz. Baileys Irish Cream

Shake first two ingredients
with ice and strain into a
shooter glass. Float Baileys on
top.

After Hours
2 oz. White Creme de Menthe
1 oz. Pepto Bismol

Shake both ingredients with
ice and strain into a shooter
glass.

After Midnight
1 oz. Coffee Liqueur
1 oz. Dark Creme de Cacao
1 oz. Cream

Shake all ingredients with ice
and strain into a shooter glass.

Afterburner
½ oz. Absolut Peppar Vodka
½ oz. Coffee Liqueur
½ oz. Cinnamon Schnapps

Shake all ingredients with ice
and strain into a shooter glass.

Afterwhile Crocodile
1 oz. Melon Liqueur
½ oz. Vodka
1 oz. Sour Mix
½ oz. Lime Juice

Shake all ingredients with ice
and strain into a shooter glass.

AK 47
½ oz. Apple Schnapps
½ oz. Light Rum
½ oz. White Sambuca
½ oz. Tequila
½ oz. Tia Maria
½ oz. Cream

Shake all ingredients with ice
and strain into a shooter glass.

Alcohol Poisoning
¾ oz. Grain Alcohol
¾ oz. Jack Daniel's
¾ oz. Peach Schnapps
¾ oz. Light Rum

Shake all ingredients with ice
and strain into a shooter glass.
Top with a sprinkle of ground
cinnamon.

Alessandro
¾ oz. White Sambuca
¾ oz. Gin
¾ oz. Cream

Shake all ingredients with ice
and strain into a shooter glass.

Alexander
½ oz. Dark Creme de Cacao
½ oz. Gin
2 oz. Cream

Shake all ingredients with ice
and strain into a shooter glass.
Top with a sprinkle of ground
nutmeg.

Alien Semen
1 oz. Sour Apple Pucker
Schnapps
1 oz. Everclear
½ oz. After Shock Cinnamon
Liqueur

Shake all ingredients with ice
and strain into a shooter glass.

Alligator on the Rag
1 oz. Melon Liqueur
½ oz. Chambord
1 oz. Jägermeister

Layer ingredients in order
given in a shooter glass.

Alligator Piss
½ oz. Southern Comfort
½ oz. Peach Schnapps
½ oz. Melon Liqueur
½ oz. Amaretto
Splash of Sour Mix

Shake all ingredients with ice
and strain into a shooter glass.

Almond Smash
1 oz. Creme de Noyeaux
½ oz. Amaretto
1 ½ oz. 7-Up

Shake all ingredients with ice
and strain into a shooter glass.

Alpine Avalanche
1 oz. Swiss Chocolate Liqueur
1 oz. Baileys Irish Cream
1 oz. Grand Marnier

Shake all ingredients with ice
and strain into a shooter glass.

Altered States
½ oz. Kahlua
½ oz. Baileys Irish Cream
½ oz. Pear Liqueur

Layer ingredients in order
given in a shooter glass.

Amaretto Chill
1 oz. Amaretto
1 oz. Vodka
1 oz. Pineapple Juice
1 oz. Lemonade

Shake all ingredients with ice
and strain into a shooter glass.

Amaretto Kamihuzi
1 oz. Amaretto
1 oz. Tequila
1 oz. Sour Mix

Shake all ingredients with ice
and strain into a shooter glass.

Amaretto Kamikaze
1 oz. Amaretto
1 oz. Vodka
½ oz. Lime Juice
½ oz. Sour Mix

Shake all ingredients with ice
and strain into a shooter glass.

Amaretto Lemondrop
1 oz. Amaretto
1 oz. Vodka
1 oz. Lemonade

Shake all ingredients with ice
and strain into a shooter glass.

Amaretto Limedrop
1 oz. Amaretto
1 oz. Vodka
1 oz. Limeade

Shake all ingredients with ice
and strain into a shooter glass.

Amaru
½ oz. After Shock Cinnamon
Liqueur
½ oz. Midori Melon Liqueur
½ oz. Blue Curacao

Layer ingredients in order
given in a shooter glass.

American Dream
¾ oz. Kahlua
¾ oz. Frangelico
¾ oz. Amaretto
¾ oz. Dark Creme de Cacao

Shake all ingredients with ice
and strain into a shooter glass.

American Flag
1 Hawaiian Punch Shooter
1 Russian Quaalude Shooter
1 Blue Hawaii Shooter

Carefully stack the glasses in
red, white, & blue order.

Amoreillo
½ oz. Amaretto di Amore
½ oz. Tequila

Combine both ingredients in a
shot glass.

Amy Girl
¾ oz. Frangelico
¾ oz. Butterscotch Schnapps
¾ oz. Creme de Banana

Layer ingredients in order
given in a shooter glass.

Anabolic Steroid
¾ oz. Blue Curacao
¾ oz. Melon Liqueur
¾ oz. Cointreau

Layer ingredients in order
given in a shooter glass.

Anal Shot
¾ oz. Jim Beam
¾ oz. Vodka
¾ oz. Milk
Dash of Grenadine

Layer ingredients in order
given in a shooter glass.

Ande's Mint
¾ oz. Kahlua
¾ oz. Peppermint Schnapps
¾ oz. Cream

Shake all ingredients with ice
and strain into a shooter glass.

Angel Bliss
½ oz. Wild Turkey Liqueur
½ oz. Bacardi 151 Rum
1 ½ oz. Blue Curacao

Layer ingredients in order
given in a shooter glass.

Angel's Dream
1 ¼ oz. Apricot Brandy
¼ oz. Cream

Layer ingredients in order
given in a shooter glass.

Angel's Tit
1 oz. Kahlua
½ oz. Baileys Irish Cream

Layer ingredients in order
given in a shooter glass.

Angry Catholic
1 oz. Tequila
4 Drops Tabasco Sauce
¼ oz. Bacardi 151 Rum

Layer ingredients in order
given in a shooter glass.
Ignite with a match.

Antifreeze
½ oz. Vodka
½ oz. Blue Curacao
½ oz. Bacardi 151 Rum
½ oz. Peppermint Schnapps

Shake all ingredients with ice
and strain into a shooter glass.

Apache
1 oz. Kahlua
1 oz. Baileys Irish Cream
1 oz. Midori Melon Liqueur

Layer ingredients in order
given in a shooter glass.

Apocalypse Now
1 oz. Baileys Irish Cream
1 oz. Dry Vermouth
1 oz. Tequila

Shake all ingredients with ice
and strain into a shooter glass.

Apple Chill
2 oz. Apple Schnapps
½ oz. Lemonade
½ oz. Pineapple Juice

Shake all ingredients with ice
and strain into a shooter glass.

Apple Cooler
1 oz. Apple Schnapps
1 oz. Orange Juice
1 oz. 7-Up

Shake all ingredients with ice
and strain into a shooter glass.

Apple Fucker
1 ½ oz. Apple Schnapps
1 ½ oz. Everclear

Shake both ingredients with
ice and strain into a shooter
glass.

Apple Kamikaze
1 oz. Apple Schnapps
1 oz. Vodka
1 oz. Sour Mix

Shake all ingredients with ice
and strain into a shooter glass.

Apple Lemondrop
1 oz. Apple Schnapps
1 oz. Vodka
1 ½ oz. Sour Mix

Shake all ingredients with ice
and strain into a shooter glass.

Apple Limedrop
1 oz. Vodka
1 oz. Apple Schnapps
1 ½ oz. Limeade

Shake all ingredients with ice
and strain into a shooter glass.

Apple Mule
½ oz. Jack Daniel's
½ oz. Southern Comfort
½ oz. Amaretto
½ oz. Triple Sec
¼ oz. Lime Juice
1 oz. Orange Juice

Shake all ingredients with ice
and strain into a shooter glass.

Apple Pie
1 ½ oz. Vodka
1 ½ oz. Apple Cider

Shake both ingredients with
ice and strain into a shooter
glass.

Apple Pie Slammer
1 oz. Captain Morgan Spiced
Rum
1 oz. Apple Juice

Shake both ingredients with
ice and strain into a shooter
glass. Top with a sprinkle of
ground cinnamon and a dash
of whipped cream.

Apple Sourball
1 oz. Vodka
1 oz. Apple Schnapps
1 oz. Lemonade
1 oz. Orange Juice

Shake all ingredients with ice
and strain into a shooter glass.

Apple-icious
1 ½ oz. Sour Apple Pucker
Schnapps
¾ oz. Vodka
1 oz. 7-Up

Shake all ingredients with ice
and strain into a shooter glass.

Apples & Oranges
1 oz. Apple Schnapps
½ oz. Orange Curacao
¾ oz. Grenadine
Juice of ½ of a Lemon

Shake all ingredients with ice
and strain into a shooter glass.

Apricot Chill
1 oz. Apricot Schnapps
1 oz. Vodka
1 oz. Lemonade
1 oz. Pineapple Juice

Shake all ingredients with ice
and strain into a shooter glass.

Apricot Cooler
1 oz. Apricot Schnapps
1 oz. Orange Juice
1 oz. 7-Up

Shake all ingredients with ice
and strain into a shooter glass.

Apricot Kamikaze
1 oz. Vodka
1 oz. Apricot Schnapps
1 oz. Sour Mix

Shake all ingredients with ice
and strain into a shooter glass.

Apricot Lemondrop
1 oz. Vodka
1 oz. Apricot Schnapps
1 oz. Lemonade

Shake all ingredients with ice
and strain into a shooter glass.

Apricot Limedrop
1 oz. Vodka
1 oz. Apricot Schnapps
1 oz. Limeade

Shake all ingredients with ice
and strain into a shooter glass.

Aquarius
1 ½ oz. Blended Whiskey
½ oz. Cherry Brandy
1 oz. Cranberry Juice

Shake all ingredients with ice
and strain into a shooter glass.

Arctic Fire
½ oz. Lupini Inferno
½ oz. Mother's Hotshots

Combine both ingredients in a
shot glass.

Are You Tough Enough?
½ oz. Firewater Cinnamon
Schnapps
½ oz. Everclear
½ oz. Ice 101 Peppermint
Schnapps
½ oz. Wild Turkey 101
½ oz. Cuervo Gold Tequila

Shake all ingredients with ice
and strain into a shooter glass.

Armadillo
¾ oz. Tequila
¾ oz. Amaretto
¾ oz. Light Rum

Shake all ingredients with ice
and strain into a shooter glass.

Armageddon
½ oz. Everclear
1 oz. Hot Damn Cinnamon
Schnapps
1 ½ oz. Southern Comfort 100
Proof

Shake all ingredients with ice
and strain into a shooter glass.

Around the World
1 oz. Gin
½ oz. Green Creme de
Menthe
1 ½ oz. Pineapple Juice

Shake all ingredients with ice
and strain into a shooter glass.

Ass Burner
2 oz. Stolichnaya Vodka
3 Dashes Tabasco Sauce
½ tsp. Ground Black Pepper
Squeeze of Fresh Lemon Juice

Shake all ingredients with ice
and strain into a shooter glass.

Ass Fucker
1 ½ oz. Grain Alcohol
2 oz. Cola
1 Package Pop Rocks Candy

Shake all ingredients with ice
and strain into a shooter glass.

Ass in a Glass
1 oz. Triple Sec
1 oz. Vodka
1 oz. Maraschino Liqueur
½ oz. Amaretto

Shake all ingredients with ice
and strain into a shooter glass.

Assisted Suicide
¾ oz. Brandy
¾ oz. Jägermeister
½ oz. Light Rum

Shake all ingredients with ice
and strain into a shooter glass.

Assmonkey
1 oz. White Creme de Menthe
1 oz. Light Creme de Cacao
½ oz. Baileys Irish Cream

Shake first two ingredients
with ice and strain into a
shooter glass. Float Baileys on
top, then sprinkle with a dash
of chocolate syrup.

Atlanta Belle
1 oz. Bourbon
¾ oz. Green Creme de
Menthe
¾ oz. Light Creme de Cacao
1 oz. Cream

Shake all ingredients with ice
and strain into a shooter glass.

Atomic Bomb
1 oz. Tequila
1 oz. Tabasco Sauce

Layer ingredients in order
given in a shooter glass.

Atomic Fireball
½ oz. Bacardi 151 Rum
½ oz. Goldschlager
½ oz. Rumple Minze
½ oz. Hot Damn Cinnamon
Schnapps
Dash of Tabasco Sauce

Shake all ingredients with ice
and strain into a shooter glass.

Aunt Jemima
1 oz. Brandy
1 oz. Dark Creme de Cacao
1 oz. Benedictine

Layer ingredients in order
given in a shooter glass.

Avas Suicide
½ oz. Vodka
¼ oz. Whiskey
¼ oz. Gin
½ oz. Pernod
½ oz. Rum
½ oz. Cherry Kool-Aid

Shake all ingredients with ice
and strain into a shooter glass.

Aviation Cocktail
1 oz. Sweet Sherry
1 oz. Dubonnet Red

Shake both ingredients with
ice and strain into a shooter
glass.

B&T
1 oz. Amaretto
1 oz. Baileys Irish Cream
1 oz. Grand Marnier

Shake all ingredients with ice
and strain into a shooter glass.

B-1
¾ oz. Kahlua
¾ oz. Frangelico
¾ oz. Drambuie

Layer ingredients in order
given in a shooter glass.

B-1 Bomber
¾ oz. Amaretto
¾ oz. Kahlua
¾ oz. Baileys Irish Cream
¾ oz. Vodka

Shake all ingredients with ice
and strain into a shooter glass.

B-52
1 oz. Kahlua
1 oz. Baileys Irish Cream
1 oz. Grand Marnier

Layer ingredients in order
given in a shooter glass.

B-52 Bomber
¾ oz. Kahlua
¾ oz. Baileys Irish Cream
¾ oz. Grand Marnier

Layer ingredients in order
given in a shooter glass.

B-52 Extreme
¾ oz. Tia Maria
¾ oz. Baileys Irish Cream
¾ oz. Grand Marnier
½ oz. Bacardi 151 Rum

Layer ingredients in order
given in a shooter glass.

B-52 with Bombay Doors
¾ oz. Kahlua
¾ oz. Bombay Sapphire Gin
¾ oz. Grand Marnier
¾ oz. Baileys Irish Cream

Shake all ingredients with ice
and strain into a shooter glass.

B-53
½ oz. Kahlua
½ oz. Baileys Irish Cream
½ oz. Amaretto
½ oz. Grand Marnier

Layer ingredients in order
given in a shooter glass.

B-54
¾ oz. Kahlua
¾ oz. Baileys Irish Cream
¾ oz. Frangelico

Layer ingredients in order
given in a shooter glass.

B-57
¾ oz. Kahlua
¾ oz. White Sambuca
¾ oz. Triple Sec

Shake all ingredients with ice
and strain into a shooter glass.

Baby Aspirin
½ oz. Absolut Mandarin
Vodka
½ oz. Absolut Citron Vodka
½ oz. Licor 43
½ oz. 7-Up

Shake all ingredients with ice
and strain into a shooter glass.
Garnish with an orange
wedge.

Baby Guinness
1 oz. Kahlua
¼ oz. Baileys Irish Cream

Layer ingredients in order
given in a shooter glass.

Baby Ruth
1 oz. Vodka
1 oz. Amaretto
3 Peanuts

Layer vodka and amaretto in a
shooter glass. Float peanuts
on top.

Bachelor's Surprise
1 oz. Kahlua
1 oz. Light Creme de Cacao
1 oz. Southern Comfort

Shake all ingredients with ice
and strain into a shooter glass.

Back Crash
1 oz. Kahlua
1 oz. Green Creme de Menthe
1 oz. Whiskey

Layer ingredients in order
given in a shooter glass.

Back to the Womb
¾ oz. Southern Comfort
¾ oz. Grand Marnier
½ oz. Jack Daniel's
½ oz. Bacardi 151 Rum

Shake all ingredients with ice
and strain into a shooter glass.

Bad Ass
1 oz. Southern Comfort
1 oz. Lime Juice

Shake both ingredients with
ice and strain into a shooter
glass.

Bad Ass Mo Fo
1 oz. Cold Beer
1 oz. Tequila
1 oz. Cold Zima

Combine all ingredients in a
shooter glass.

Bahama Mama
1 oz. Malibu Rum
½ oz. Cherry Brandy
1 oz. Orange Juice
1 oz. Pineapple Juice

Shake all ingredients with ice
and strain into a shooter glass.

Baileys Byte
1 ½ oz. Baileys Irish Cream
1 ½ oz. Vodka

Shake both ingredients with
ice and strain into a shooter
glass.

**Baileys Chocolate Covered
Cherry**
½ oz. Grenadine
1 oz. Kahlua
1 oz. Baileys Irish Cream

Layer ingredients in order
given in a shooter glass.

Baileys Sunset
¾ oz. Kahlua
¾ oz. Baileys Irish Cream
¾ oz. Triple Sec

Layer ingredients in order
given in a shooter glass.

Baker's Delight
1 oz. Peach Schnapps
1 ½ oz. Light Creme de Cacao

Shake both ingredients with
ice and strain into a shooter
glass.

Bald Women
1 ½ oz. Bacardi 151 Rum
½ oz. Grapefruit Juice
½ oz. Cranberry Juice

Shake both ingredients with
ice and strain into a shooter
glass.

Bald-Headed Woman
1 ½ oz. Bacardi 151 Rum
½ oz. Grapefruit Juice

Shake both ingredients with
ice and strain into a shooter
glass.

Ball Banger
1 ½ oz. Ouzo
1 ½ oz. Orange Juice

Shake both ingredients with
ice and strain into a shooter
glass.

Ballistic Missile
1 oz. Amaretto
1 oz. Grand Marnier
1 oz. Pineapple Juice

Shake all ingredients with ice
and strain into a shooter glass.

Baltimore Bean
½ oz. Anisette
½ oz. Southern Comfort
¼ oz. Grenadine

Shake all ingredients with ice and strain into a large shot glass.

Bambi
¾ oz. Kahlua
1 ¼ oz. Baileys Irish Cream
Dash of Courvoisier VS

Shake all ingredients with ice and strain into a shooter glass.

Banana Beef Brownie
1 oz. Creme de Banana
1 Beef Bouillon Cube

Combine both ingredients in a shot glass.

Banana Bomber
1 oz. Creme de Banana
1 oz. Brandy

Layer ingredients in order given in a shooter glass.

Banana Chill
1 oz. Banana Schnapps
1 oz. Vodka
1 oz. Sour Mix
1 oz. Pineapple Juice

Shake all ingredients with ice and strain into a shooter glass.

Banana Cooler
1 oz. Banana Schnapps
1 oz. Orange Juice
1 oz. 7-Up

Shake all ingredients with ice and strain into a shooter glass.

Banana Cream Pie
1 oz. Malibu Rum
1 oz. Creme de Banana
1 oz. Cream

Shake all ingredients with ice and strain into a shooter glass.

Banana Flips
1 ½ oz. Creme de Banana
1 ½ oz. Cream

Shake both ingredients with ice and strain into a shooter glass.

Banana Kamikaze
1 oz. Banana Schnapps
1 oz. Vodka
1 oz. Sour Mix

Shake all ingredients with ice and strain into a shooter glass.

Banana Lemondrop
1 oz. Banana Schnapps
1 oz. Vodka
1 oz. Lemonade

Shake all ingredients with ice and strain into a shooter glass.

Banana Limedrop
1 oz. Banana Schnapps
1 oz. Vodka
1 oz. Limeade

Shake all ingredients with ice and strain into a shooter glass.

Banana Loco
¾ oz. Kahlua
¾ oz. Creme de Banana
¾ oz. Cream

Layer ingredients in order given in a shooter glass.

Banana Moo
1 ½ oz. Creme de Banana
1 ½ oz. Cream

Shake both ingredients with ice and strain into a shooter glass.

Banana Slip
1 ½ oz. Creme de Banana
1 ½ oz. Baileys Irish Cream

Layer ingredients in order given in a shooter glass.

Banana Split
¾ oz. Kahlua
¾ oz. Malibu Rum
¾ oz. Creme de Banana
¾ oz. Pineapple Juice

Shake all ingredients with ice and strain into a shooter glass.

Bandera
1 oz. Silver Tequila
1 oz. Lime Juice
1 oz. Tomato Juice

Pour each ingredient into a
separate shot glass. Drink in
order.

Bandido
1 ½ oz. Kahlua
1 ½ oz. Sauza Gold Tequila

Shake both ingredients with
ice and strain into a shooter
glass.

Bar Time
1 oz. Vandermint Liqueur
1 oz. Amaretto
1 oz. Vodka
½ oz. Cream

Shake all ingredients with ice
and strain into a shooter glass.

Barbarella
2 oz. Cointreau
1 oz. White Sambuca

Shake both ingredients with
ice and strain into a shooter
glass.

Barfing Sensations
½ oz. Blackberry Liqueur
½ oz. Peach Schnapps
½ oz. Vodka
½ oz. Applejack
½ oz. Raspberry Schnapps

Shake all ingredients with ice
and strain into a shooter glass.

Barium Enema
1 oz. Vodka
3 oz. Club Soda
1 tsp. Metamucil Powder

Combine all ingredients in a
shooter glass and stir well.

Barking Spider
½ oz. Kahlua
½ oz. Peppermint Schnapps
½ oz. Tequila

Layer ingredients in order
given in a shooter glass.

Barmida Shooter
1 oz. Gin
1 oz. Apricot Brandy
1 oz. Sour Mix
¼ oz. Triple Sec
Dash of Grenadine

Shake all ingredients with ice
and strain into a shooter glass.

Barney Shot
½ oz. Cinnamon Schnapps
½ oz. Avalanche Blue
Peppermint Schnapps

Combine both ingredients in a
shot glass.

Barnum & Bailey
2 oz. Baileys Irish Cream
½ oz. Apricot Brandy

Shake both ingredients with
ice and strain into a shooter
glass. Float ½ of a cherry and
2 miniature marshmallows on
top to form a clown face.

Bart Simpson
½ oz. Crown Royal
½ oz. Amaretto
½ oz. Peach Schnapps
½ oz. Cranberry Juice

Shake all ingredients with ice
and strain into a shooter glass.

Bass Tackler
1 oz. Cinnamon Schnapps
1 oz. Apple Schnapps
1 oz. Grain Alcohol

Shake all ingredients with ice
and strain into a shooter glass.

Bassmaster
1 oz. Galliano
2 oz. Grain Alcohol
¼ oz. Lemon Juice
¼ oz. Grapefruit Juice
Pinch of Salt

Shake all ingredients with ice
and strain into a shooter glass.

Battery Acid
1 oz. Cuervo Gold Tequila
1 oz. Grand Marnier

Shake both ingredients with
ice and strain into a shooter
glass.

Bazooka Joe
1 oz. Creme de Banana
1 oz. Baileys Irish Cream
1 oz. Parfait Amour

Shake all ingredients with ice
and strain into a shooter glass.

Be Right Back
½ oz. Jim Beam
½ oz. Malibu Rum
½ oz. Baileys Irish Cream

Layer ingredients in order given in a shooter glass. Top with whipped cream and a dash of Grenadine.

Beach Blanket
1 oz. Rum
1 oz. Southern Comfort
½ oz. Orange Curacao
½ oz. Sour Mix

Shake all ingredients with ice and strain into a shooter glass.

Beachcomber
1 oz. Vodka
1 oz. Raspberry Schnapps
½ oz. Sour Mix
½ oz. Lime Juice
½ oz. Cranberry Juice

Shake all ingredients with ice and strain into a shooter glass.

Beached Whale
1 ¼ oz. Light Creme de Cacao
1 ¼ oz. Cointreau
½ oz. Advocaat

Shake all ingredients with ice and strain into a shooter glass.

Beam Me Up, Scotty
1 oz. Baileys Irish Cream
1 oz. Creme de Banana
1 oz. Kahlua

Shake all ingredients with ice and strain into a shooter glass.

Beam Scream
1 oz. Jim Beam
1 oz. After Shock

Shake both ingredients with ice and strain into a shooter glass.

Beautiful Oblivion
½ oz. After Shock Cinnamon Liqueur
½ oz. Rumple Minze
½ oz. Goldschlager

Layer ingredients in order given in a shooter glass.

Beaver Blast
¾ oz. Bacardi Limon Rum
¾ oz. Captain Morgan Spiced Rum
¾ oz. Malibu Rum

Shake all ingredients with ice and strain into a shooter glass.

Beavis & Butthead
½ oz. Apple Schnapps
½ oz. Cinnamon Schnapps

Combine both ingredients in a shot glass. Top with a dash of whipped cream.

Bee Sting
1 ½ oz. Tequila Silver
¼ oz. Yellow Chartreuse

Layer ingredients in order given in a shooter glass.

Beer Nuts
1 oz. Frangelico
1 oz. Root Beer Schnapps

Shake both ingredients with ice and strain into a shooter glass.

Bee's Kiss
2 oz. Rum
½ oz. Cream
½ oz. Honey

Shake all ingredients with ice and strain into a shooter glass.

Belfast Bomber
1 ½ oz. Hennessy VS
1 ½ oz. Baileys Irish Cream

Shake all ingredients with ice and strain into a shooter glass.

Belize Breeze
1 oz. Tequila
1 oz. Amaretto

Shake both ingredients with ice and strain into a shooter glass.

Benson Bomber
¼ oz. Vodka
¼ oz. Brandy
¼ oz. Kahlua
¼ oz. Amaretto
¼ oz. Dark Creme de Cacao
Splash of Cola
½ oz. Cream

Shake all ingredients with ice and strain into a shooter glass. Float an additional ½ oz. cream on top.

Beowulf
1 ½ oz. Blue Curacao
1 ½ oz. Vodka

Shake both ingredients with
ice and strain into a shooter
glass.

Berry Berry Best
1 oz. Blackberry Brandy
1 oz. Vodka
1 oz. Sour Mix

Shake all ingredients with ice
and strain into a shooter glass.

Berry Blast
1 ½ oz. Vodka
1 ½ oz. Strawberry Juice

Shake both ingredients with
ice and strain into a shooter
glass.

Berry Comfortable
1 oz. Southern Comfort
1 oz. Amaretto
1 ½ oz. Cranberry Juice

Shake all ingredients with ice
and strain into a shooter glass.
Top with a splash of club
soda.

Better Than Sex
½ oz. Frangelico
½ oz. Haagen-Dazs Cream
Liqueur
¼ oz. Grand Marnier
½ oz. Kahlua
¾ oz. Cream

Shake all ingredients with ice
and strain into a shooter glass.

Beverly Hills
¾ oz. Creme de Banana
¾ oz. Triple Sec
¾ oz. Grand Marnier

Shake all ingredients with ice
and strain into a shooter glass.

Big Ben
1 oz. Creme de Banana
1 oz. Baileys Irish Cream
1 oz. Brandy

Shake all ingredients with ice
and strain into a shooter glass.

Big Fat One
¾ oz. Melon Liqueur
¾ oz. Vodka
¾ oz. Triple Sec
¾ oz. Orange Juice

Shake all ingredients with ice
and strain into a shooter glass.

Big Lebowski
1 oz. Amaretto
1 oz. Vodka
1 oz. Cream

Shake all ingredients with ice
and strain into a shooter glass.

Big Roller
1 oz. Kahlua
1 oz. Creme de Banana
1 oz. Amaretto

Shake all ingredients with ice
and strain into a shooter glass.
Float ½ of a cherry on top.

Bikini
1 oz. Strawberry Liqueur
1 oz. Grand Marnier
1 oz. Vodka

Shake all ingredients with ice
and strain into a shooter glass.

Bikini Line
1 oz. Tia Maria
1 oz. Vodka
1 oz. Chambord

Shake all ingredients with ice
and strain into a shooter glass.

Billy Bad Ass
1 oz. Bacardi 151 Rum
1 oz. Tequila
1 oz. Jägermeister

Shake all ingredients with ice
and strain into a shooter glass.

Billy Beer
1 ½ oz. Licor 43
½ oz. Heavy Cream

Layer ingredients in order
given in a shooter glass. Top
with a cherry.

Bird's Nest
1 oz. Gin
½ oz. Anisette
1 oz. Cream
½ of an Egg White

Shake all ingredients with ice
and strain into a shooter glass.

Biscuit Neck
¾ oz. Amaretto
¾ oz. Wild Turkey 101
¾ oz. Frangelico
¾ oz. Baileys Irish Cream

Shake all ingredients with ice
and strain into a shooter glass.

Bitch
½ oz. Chambord
½ oz. Vodka
½ oz. Rum
¼ oz. Pineapple Juice
¼ oz. Orange Juice

Shake all ingredients with ice
and strain into a shooter glass.

**Bitch in Heat in the Back
Seat**
1 oz. Southern Comfort
1 oz. Captain Morgan Spiced
Rum
1 oz. Pineapple Juice
Splash of Ginger Ale

Shake all ingredients with ice
and strain into a shooter glass.

Bitch on the Wet Spot
¾ oz. Peach Schnapps
¾ oz. Melon Liqueur
¾ oz. Orange Juice
¾ oz. Cream

Shake all ingredients with ice
and strain into a shooter glass.

Bitter Bikini
1 ½ oz. Campari
1 oz. Dry Vermouth
½ oz. Triple Sec

Shake all ingredients with ice
and strain into a shooter glass.

Black & Gold
1 oz. Goldschlager
1 oz. Jägermeister

Layer ingredients in order
given in a shooter glass.

Black Baby
1 oz. Kahlua
1 oz. Cream
1 oz. Cola

Layer ingredients in order
given in a shooter glass.

Black Banana
1 oz. Kahlua
1 oz. Creme de Banana
1 oz. Vodka

Shake all ingredients with ice
and strain into a shooter glass.

Black Bullet
1 oz. Jägermeister
1 oz. Peppermint Schnapps

Layer ingredients in order
given in a shooter glass.

Black Cat
1 oz. Anisette
1 oz. Parfait Amour
1 oz. Tequila

Shake all ingredients with ice
and strain into a shooter glass.

Black Dragon
¾ oz. Kahlua
¾ oz. Peppermint Schnapps
¾ oz. Scotch

Combine all ingredients in a
shooter glass.

Black Forest
1 oz. Kahlua
1 oz. Cherry Brandy
1 oz. Baileys Irish Cream

Shake all ingredients with ice
and strain into a shooter glass.

Black Hole
1 oz. Jägermeister
1 oz. Rumple Minze

Chill each ingredient
separately with ice. Strain the
Jägermeister into a shooter
glass, then strain the Rumple
Minze into the center of the
Jägermeister.

Black Jelly Bean
1 oz. Parfait Amour
1 oz. Anisette

Shake both ingredients with
ice and strain into a shooter
glass.

Black Kentucky
1 oz. Black Sambuca
1 oz. Rye Whiskey

Layer ingredients in order
given in a shooter glass.

Black Knight Mars Bar
¾ oz. Baileys Irish Cream
¾ oz. Frangelico
¾ oz. Kahlua

Shake all ingredients with ice
and strain into a shooter glass.
Top with whipped cream and
shaved dark chocolate.

Black M&M
¼ oz. Brandy
½ oz. Rum
¾ oz. Tequila
1 oz. Whiskey

Shake all ingredients with ice
and strain into a shooter glass.
Drop an M&M candy into the
drink.

Black Man
1 oz. Tia Maria
1 oz. Jack Daniel's

Layer ingredients in order
given in a shooter glass.

Black Orchid
¾ oz. Tequila
½ oz. Chambord
½ oz. Blue Curacao
Dash of Cranberry Juice
Dash of Lime Juice

Shake all ingredients with ice
and strain into a shooter glass.

Black Orgasm
½ oz. Blue Curacao
½ oz. Peach Schnapps
½ oz. Sloe Gin
½ oz. Vodka

Shake all ingredients with ice
and strain into a shooter glass.

Black Peppar
1 ¼ oz. Absolut Peppar
Vodka
¼ oz. Blackberry Brandy

Shake both ingredients with
ice and strain into a large shot
glass.

Black Sabbath
1 oz. Jack Daniel's
1 oz. Light Rum
1 oz. Jägermeister

Shake all ingredients with ice
and strain into a shooter glass.

Black Tie
1 oz. Drambuie
1 oz. Scotch
1 oz. Parfait Amour

Shake all ingredients with ice
and strain into a shooter glass.

Black Tooth
1 oz. Jack Daniel's
3 Drops Cola

Pour Jack Daniel's into a shot
glass. Top with the three
drops of cola.

Bleacher Twist
1 oz. Coffee Liqueur
1 oz. Baileys Irish Cream
1 oz. Chambord

Layer ingredients in order
given in a shooter glass.

Bleeding Heart
1 oz. Advocaat
1 oz. Cherry Brandy

Layer ingredients in order
given in a shooter glass.

Blitz
¾ oz. Baileys Irish Cream
¾ oz. Tia Maria
¾ oz. Pineapple Juice

Shake all ingredients with ice
and strain into a shooter glass.

Blonde Bombshell
1 oz. Vodka
1 oz. Brandy
¼ oz. Apple Schnapps
¼ oz. Pear Schnapps

Shake all ingredients with ice
and strain into a shooter glass.

Blonde Ponani
1 oz. Baileys Irish Cream
1 oz. Vodka
½ oz. Malibu Rum

Shake all ingredients with ice
and strain into a shooter glass.

Blood & Guts
1 ½ oz. Chilled White
Zinfandel
Dash of Baileys Irish Cream

Pour wine into a shooter glass
and slowly add the Baileys.

Blood Clot
½ oz. Amaretto
½ oz. Southern Comfort
1 oz. 7-Up
Dash of Grenadine

Place a shot glass into a
shooter glass. Into the shooter
glass, pour the Amaretto and
the Southern Comfort. Into
the shot glass, pour the
Grenadine. Fill with 7-Up.

Bloodeye
1 oz. Absolut Citron Vodka
¾ oz. Raspberry Liqueur
¾ oz. Cranberry Cordial

Layer ingredients in order
given in a shooter glass.

Bloody Brain
1 oz. Strawberry Schnapps
½ oz. Baileys Irish Cream

Pour schnapps in a shooter glass. Pour Baileys in the center of the schnapps. Top with a dash of Grenadine.

Bloody Fetus
1 ¼ oz. Baileys Irish Cream
Dash of Grenadine

Layer ingredients in order given in a shooter glass.

Bloody Indian Fart
1 ¼ oz. Tequila
¼ oz. Tabasco Sauce
¼ oz. Worcestershire Sauce

Layer ingredients in order given in a shooter glass.

Bloody Orgasm
1 oz. Kahlua
1 oz. Amaretto
¾ oz. Baileys Irish Cream

Shake all ingredients with ice and strain into a shooter glass. Top with a dash of Grenadine.

Bloody Patriot Eyes
2 oz. Vodka
2 oz. Pineapple Juice
1 ½ oz. Coco Lopez

Combine all ingredients in a blender with a scoop of ice. Process until smooth. Pour into two separate shooter glasses. Float ¼ oz. Parfait Amour on top of each

Bloody Pineapple
1 oz. Finlandia Pineapple Vodka
½ oz. Blue Curacao
1 oz. Pineapple Juice
1 tsp. Sugar

Combine all ingredients in a blender with a scoop of ice. Process until smooth. Pour into a shooter glass. Top with ¼ oz. Grenadine.

Blow Job
1 oz. Baileys Irish Cream
1 oz. Grand Marnier
1 oz. Creme de Banana

Combine all ingredients in a shooter glass.

Blue Balls
1 oz. Vodka
½ oz. Lime Juice
½ oz. Triple Sec
½ oz. Blue Curacao

Shake all ingredients with ice and strain into a shooter glass.

Blue Bastard
1 ½ oz. Triple Sec
1 oz. Blueberry Schnapps
½ oz. Lime Juice
1 tbs. Sugar

Shake all ingredients with ice and strain into a shooter glass.

Blue Blood
1 ½ oz. Vodka
¾ oz. Blue Curacao

Shake both ingredients with ice and strain into a shooter glass.

Blue Burner
1 ¼ oz. Absolut Peppar Vodka
½ oz. Blue Curacao

Shake both ingredients with ice and strain into a shooter glass.

Blue Cocaine
1 oz. Vodka
1 oz. Blue Curacao
½ oz. Lime Juice
½ oz. Water

Shake all ingredients with ice and strain into a shooter glass.

Blue Devil
1 ¼ oz. Gin
½ oz. Blue Curacao
½ oz. Sour Mix

Shake all ingredients with ice and strain into a shooter glass.

Blue Eyed Blonde
1 oz. Blue Curacao
1 oz. Creme de Banana

Layer ingredients in order given in a shooter glass.

Blue Eyed Canadian Whore With A Touch of Gold
¾ oz. Canadian Club
¾ oz. Skyy Vodka
¾ oz. Goldschlager

Layer ingredients in order given in a shooter glass.

Blue Flame
¾ oz. Galliano
¾ oz. Southern Comfort
½ oz. Grenadine
½ oz. Green Chartreuse

Shake first three ingredients
with ice and strain into a
shooter glass. Float Green
Chartreuse on top and light
with a match.

Blue Hawaii
1 oz. Malibu Rum
1 oz. Parfait Amour

Shake both ingredients with
ice and strain into a shooter
glass.

Blue Hawaiian Punch
1 oz. Blue Curacao
1 oz. Malibu Rum
1 oz. Pineapple Juice

Shake all ingredients with ice
and strain into a shooter glass.

Blue Ice
1 oz. White Creme de Menthe
1 oz. Peppermint Schnapps
1 oz. Parfait Amour

Shake all ingredients with ice
and strain into a shooter glass.

Blue Jay
1 oz. Parfait Amour
1 oz. Peppermint Schnapps
1 oz. Creme de Banana

Shake all ingredients with ice
and strain into a shooter glass.

Blue Jesus
¾ oz. Kahlua
¾ oz. Baileys Irish Cream
¾ oz. Bacardi 151 Rum

Layer ingredients in order
given in a shooter glass.
Ignite with a match.

Blue Kamikaze
1 ½ oz. Vodka
¾ oz. Blue Curacao
½ oz. Lime Juice

Shake both ingredients with
ice and strain into a shooter
glass.

Blue Lamborghini
1 oz. Blue Curacao
1 oz. Bacardi 151 Rum

Combine both ingredients in a
shooter glass. Ignite with a
match.

Blue Marlin
1 oz. Rum
1 oz. Blue Curacao
1 oz. Lime Juice

Shake all ingredients with ice
and strain into a shooter glass.

Blue Monday
2 oz. Vodka
1 oz. Cointreau
½ oz. Blue Curacao

Shake all ingredients with ice
and strain into a shooter glass.

Blue Mother Fucker
1 oz. Blue Curacao
1 oz. Everclear

Shake both ingredients with
ice and strain into a shooter
glass.

Blue Motorcycle
½ oz. Vodka
½ oz. Gin
½ oz. Rum
½ oz. Blue Curacao
½ oz. Sour Mix
½ oz. 7-Up

Shake all ingredients with ice
and strain into a shooter glass.

Blue Popper
1 oz. Blue Curacao
1 oz. Absolut Peppar Vodka

Shake both ingredients with
ice and strain into a shooter
glass.

Blue Shark
1 oz. Tequila
1 oz. Vodka
¾ oz. Blue Curacao

Shake all ingredients with ice
and strain into a shooter glass.

Blue Spruce
1 ½ oz. Vodka
1 oz. Maple Syrup

Shake both ingredients
without ice and strain into a
shooter glass.

Blue VW Bus
¾ oz. Vodka
¾ oz. Rumple Minze
¾ oz. Goldschlager
¼ oz. Blue Curacao

Shake all ingredients with ice
and strain into a shooter glass.

Blue Whale
1 oz. Blue Curacao
½ oz. Apricot Brandy
½ oz. Triple Sec
½ oz. Pineapple Juice
½ oz. Sour Mix

Shake all ingredients with ice
and strain into a shooter glass.

Blueberry Cheesecake
1 oz. Blueberry Schnapps
1 oz. Baileys Irish Cream
½ oz. Cream
½ oz. Vodka

Shake all ingredients with ice
and strain into a shooter glass.

Blueberry Chill
1 oz. Blueberry Schnapps
1 oz. Vodka
1 oz. Lemonade
1 oz. Pineapple Juice

Shake all ingredients with ice
and strain into a shooter glass.

Blueberry Cooler
1 oz. Blueberry Schnapps
1 oz. Vodka
1 oz. Orange Juice
1 oz. 7-Up

Shake all ingredients with ice
and strain into a shooter glass.

Blueberry Kamikaze
1 oz. Vodka
1 oz. Blueberry Schnapps
1 oz. Sour Mix

Shake all ingredients with ice
and strain into a shooter glass.

Blueberry Lemondrop
1 oz. Blueberry Schnapps
1 oz. Vodka
1 oz. Lemonade

Shake all ingredients with ice
and strain into a shooter glass.

Blueberry Limedrop
1 oz. Blueberry Schnapps
1 oz. Vodka
1 oz. Limeade

Shake all ingredients with ice
and strain into a shooter glass.

Blur
1 oz. Bacardi 151 Rum
1 oz. Goldschlager

Shake both ingredients with
ice and strain into a shooter
glass.

Blushin' Russian
2 oz. Vodka
1 oz. Chambord
½ oz. Lime Juice

Shake all ingredients with ice
and strain into a shooter glass.

Bo Diddley
¾ oz. Ouzo
¾ oz. Baileys Irish Cream

Layer ingredients in order
given in a shooter glass.

Bob Marley
¾ oz. Kahlua
¾ oz. Midori Melon Liqueur
¾ oz. Grain Alcohol

Layer ingredients in order
given in a shooter glass.

Body Chemistry
1 ½ oz. Southern Comfort
1 ½ oz. Cranberry Juice
¼ oz. Lime Juice

Shake all ingredients with ice
and strain into a shooter glass.

Bog in a Bowl
1 oz. Dark Rum
1 oz. Midori Melon Liqueur
1 oz. Orange Juice

Shake all ingredients with ice
and strain into a shooter glass.
Garnish with a chocolate chip
speared with a toothpick.

Bong Water
1 oz. Jägermeister
1 oz. Melon Liqueur
1 oz. Orange Juice

Shake all ingredients with ice
and strain into a shooter glass.

Bonsai Pipeline
1 oz. Maui Tropical Schnapps
½ oz. Vodka

Shake both ingredients with
ice and strain into a shooter
glass.

Booger
½ oz. Malibu Rum
½ oz. Creme de Banana
½ oz. Midori Melon Liqueur

Shake all ingredients with ice and strain into a shooter glass. Top with one drop of Baileys Irish Cream.

Boogers in the Grass
1 oz. Melon Liqueur
1 oz. Peach Schnapps

Combine both ingredients in a shooter glass. Top with one drop of Baileys Irish Cream.

Boomer
½ oz. Rum
½ oz. Creme de Banana
½ oz. Pineapple Juice
½ oz. Orange Juice

Shake all ingredients with ice and strain into a shooter glass.

Boot Hill
1 ½ oz. Blended Whiskey
½ oz. Applejack
1 oz. Sour Mix

Shake all ingredients with ice and strain into a shooter glass.

Boston Cocktail
1 oz. Gin
1 oz. Apricot Brandy
Dash of Grenadine
Dash of Sour Mix

Shake all ingredients with ice and strain into a shooter glass.

Bottom Bouncer
1 oz. Baileys Irish Cream
1 oz. Butterscotch Schnapps

Shake both ingredients with ice and strain into a shooter glass.

Brain
¾ oz. Peach Schnapps
¼ oz. Baileys Irish Cream
Dash of Grenadine

Combine all ingredients in a shot glass.

Brain Damage
1 ½ oz. Peach Schnapps
¼ oz. Baileys Irish Cream

Layer ingredients in order given in a shooter glass. Top with a dash of Grenadine.

Brain Eraser
1 oz. Everclear
¾ oz. Whiskey
½ oz. Tequila
¼ oz. Vodka
¼ oz. Rum

Shake all ingredients with ice and strain into a shooter glass.

Brain Fart
½ oz. Peach Schnapps
¼ oz. Kahlua
¼ oz. Crown Royal
Dash of Grenadine

Shake all ingredients with ice and strain into a shooter glass. Float ½ oz. Baileys Irish Cream on top.

Brain Hemorrhage
¾ oz. Vodka
¾ oz. Gin
¾ oz. Tequila
¼ oz. Baileys Irish Cream
Dash of Grenadine

Shake vodka, gin, and tequila with ice and strain into a shooter glass. Drop in a cocktail olive. Float Baileys on top and add Grenadine.

Brain Teaser
1 oz. Amaretto
1 oz. Sloe Gin
1 oz. Baileys Irish Cream

Shake all ingredients with ice and strain into a shooter glass.

Brain Tumor
2 oz. Baileys Irish Cream
¼ oz. Strawberry Schnapps

Pour Baileys into a shooter glass. Pour schnapps into the center of the Baileys.

Brainstorm
1 ¼ oz. Baileys Irish Cream
½ oz. Cinnamon Schnapps

Layer ingredients in order given in a shooter glass.

British Clusterfuck
1 oz. Gin
1 oz. Scotch
1 oz. Baileys Irish Cream

Shake all ingredients with ice and strain into a shooter glass.

Broken Down Golf Cart
1 oz. Amaretto
1 oz. Melon Liqueur
Splash of Cranberry Juice

Shake all ingredients with ice
and strain into a shooter glass.

Brown Eyed Girl
1 oz. Vodka
1 oz. Sour Mix
1 oz. 7-Up
1 oz. Cola

Shake all ingredients with ice
and strain into a shooter glass.

BS 2
¾ oz. Coffee Liqueur
¾ oz. Grand Marnier
¾ oz. Baileys Irish Cream

Shake all ingredients with ice
and strain into a shooter glass.

Bubble Gum
1 oz. Creme de Banana
1 oz. Southern Comfort
1 oz. Cream
Dash of Grenadine

Shake all ingredients with ice
and strain into a shooter glass.

Bubbly Row Slammer
2 oz. Vodka
1 Alka Seltzer Tablet

Chill vodka with ice and
strain into a shooter glass.
Add Alka Seltzer tablet.

Buca Bear
1 ¼ oz. White Sambuca
1 ¼ oz. Root Beer Schnapps

Layer ingredients in order
given in a shooter glass.

Buckaroo Bonzai
1 ½ oz. Wild Turkey
½ oz. Plum Wine

Layer ingredients in order
given in a shooter glass.

Buffalo Sweat
¾ oz. Bacardi 151 Rum
¾ oz. Tabasco Sauce

Stir both ingredients with ice
and strain into a shooter glass.

Bum Fucker
1 ½ oz. Jack Daniel's
1 ½ oz. Tequila

Stir both ingredients with ice
and strain into a shooter glass.

Bumble Bee
¾ oz. Creme de Banana
¾ oz. Tia Maria
¾ oz. Triple Sec

Layer ingredients in order
given in a shooter glass.

Burn Doctor
1 oz. Hot Damn Cinnamon
Schnapps
1 oz. Dr. Pepper

Combine both ingredients in a
shooter glass.

Burning Banana Boat
1 oz. Creme de Banana
1 oz. Kahlua

Shake both ingredients with
ice and strain into a shooter
glass. Float ½ oz. Bacardi 151
Rum on top. Light with a
match.

Burnt Embers
1 oz. Rum
1 oz. Apricot Schnapps
1 oz. Pineapple Juice

Shake all ingredients with ice
and strain into a shooter glass.

Busted Brownie
1 oz. Bourbon
1 oz. Dark Creme de Cacao
1 oz. Cream

Shake all ingredients with ice
and strain into a shooter glass.

Busted Nuts
½ oz. Vodka
½ oz. Kahlua
½ oz. Frangelico
½ oz. Amaretto
½ oz. Cream

Shake all ingredients with ice
and strain into a shooter glass.

Butt Crack
1 ½ oz. Absolut Citron Vodka
1 oz. Red Rum

Shake both ingredients with
ice and strain into a shooter
glass.

Butt Fucks
1 oz. Amaretto
1 oz. Southern Comfort
½ oz. Yukon Jack
½ oz. Lime Juice

Shake all ingredients with ice
and strain into a shooter glass.

Butter Baby
½ oz. Baileys Irish Cream
½ oz. Butterscotch Schnapps

Layer ingredients in order
given in a shot glass.

Butterball
1 oz. Butterscotch Schnapps
½ oz. Baileys Irish Cream

Layer ingredients in order
given in a shooter glass.

Butterball Turkey
¾ oz. Wild Turkey
¾ oz. Butterscotch Schnapps
1 ½ oz. Cream

Shake all ingredients with ice
and strain into a shooter glass.

Buttercup
½ oz. Butterscotch Schnapps
1 oz. Truffles Liqueur
1 ½ oz. Cream

Shake all ingredients with ice
and strain into a shooter glass.
Top with a dash of whipped
cream.

Butterscotch Fizz
1 ½ oz. Butterscotch
Schnapps
1 oz. Vodka
1 oz. Cream

Shake all ingredients with ice
and strain into a shooter glass.

Butterscotch Slide
1 oz. Baileys Irish Cream
1 oz. Kahlua
1 oz. Butterscotch Schnapps
1 oz. Cream

Shake all ingredients with ice
and strain into a shooter glass.

Buttery Nipple
1 ½ oz. Baileys Irish Cream
1 ½ oz. Butterscotch
Schnapps

Shake both ingredients with
ice and strain into a shooter
glass.

Buzzard's Breath
1 oz. Amaretto
1 oz. Peppermint Schnapps
1 oz. Coffee Liqueur

Shake all ingredients with ice
and strain into a shooter glass.

By The Pool
1 oz. Vodka
1 oz. Peach Schnapps
½ oz. Melon Liqueur
½ oz. Orange Juice
½ oz. 7-Up

Shake all ingredients with ice
and strain into a shooter glass.

C.C. Kazi
1 ½ oz. Tequila
1 ½ oz. Cranberry Juice
¼ oz. Lime Juice

Shake all ingredients with ice
and strain into a shooter glass.

Ca-Ca
¾ oz. Cafe Royale
¾ oz. Anisette
¾ oz. Cherry Brandy
¾ oz. Amaretto

Shake all ingredients with ice
and strain into a shooter glass.

Cactus Bite
1 oz. Tequila
¼ oz. Triple Sec
¼ oz. Drambuie
1 oz. Lemon Juice
1 tsp. Sugar
Dash of Bitters

Shake all ingredients with ice
and strain into a shooter glass.

Cafe d'Almond
1 oz. Coffee Liqueur
1 oz. Amaretto
2 oz. Cream

Shake all ingredients with ice
and strain into a shooter glass.

Cahoots Shooter
1 oz. Gin
1 oz. Cherry Brandy
½ oz. Triple Sec
½ oz. Pineapple Juice

Shake all ingredients with ice
and strain into a shooter glass.

California Kamikaze
1 oz. Vodka
1 oz. Lime Juice
½ oz. Triple Sec
½ oz. Grand Marnier

Shake all ingredients with ice
and strain into a shooter glass.

Cam Shaft
¾ oz. Baileys Irish Cream
¾ oz. Jägermeister
¾ oz. Root Beer Schnapps

Shake all ingredients with ice
and strain into a shooter glass.

Canadian Stone Fence
1 ½ oz. Canadian Whisky
½ oz. Triple Sec
2 oz. Apple Cider
Dash of Simple Syrup

Shake all ingredients with ice
and strain into a shooter glass.

Candy Cane
½ oz. Grenadine
½ oz. Green Creme de
Menthe
½ oz. Peppermint Schnapps

Layer ingredients in order
given in a shooter glass.

Candy Raccoon
1 oz. Goldschlager
1 oz. Black Sambuca

Combine both ingredients in a
shooter glass.

Capri
1 oz. Light Creme de Cacao
1 oz. Creme de Banana
1 oz. Cream

Shake all ingredients with ice
and strain into a shooter glass.

Caramel Apple
1 oz. Butterscotch Schnapps
1 oz. Sour Apple Pucker
Schnapps

Shake both ingredients with
ice and strain into a shooter
glass.

Caribbean Quaalude
½ oz. Baileys Irish Cream
1 oz. Amaretto
1 oz. Light Creme de Cacao
1 oz. Malibu Rum

Shake all ingredients with ice
and strain into a shooter glass.

Caribbean Shooter
¾ oz. Captain Morgan Spiced
Rum
½ oz. Brandy
1 oz. Cranberry Juice

Shake all ingredients with ice
and strain into a shooter glass.

Caribbean Summer
1 oz. 99 Bananas
1 oz. Malibu Rum
1 oz. Pineapple Juice

Shake all ingredients with ice
and strain into a shooter glass.

Carmalita
¾ oz. Baileys Irish Cream
¾ oz. Frangelico
¾ oz. Kahlua
¾ oz. Absolut Vodka

Shake all ingredients with ice
and strain into a shooter glass.

Carmel Apple
1 ½ oz. Butterscotch
Schnapps
1 ½ oz. Sour Apple Pucker
Schnapps

Layer ingredients in order
given in a shooter glass.

Carrot Cake
¾ oz. Butterscotch Schnapps
½ oz. Cinnamon Schnapps
¾ oz. Baileys Irish Cream

Layer ingredients in order
given in a shooter glass.

Cat's Claw
1 ½ oz. Jägermeister
1 ½ oz. Hot Damn Cinnamon
Schnapps

Layer ingredients in order
given in a shooter glass.

Celtic Comrade
½ oz. Kahlua
½ oz. Vodka
½ oz. Baileys Irish Cream
½ oz. Drambuie

Layer ingredients in order
given in a shooter glass.

Celtic Warrior
¾ oz. Jameson Irish Whiskey
¼ oz. Baileys Irish Cream

Shake both ingredients with
ice and strain into a shot glass.

Cement Mixer
1 ½ oz. Baileys Irish Cream
¼ oz. Lime Juice

Combine both ingredients in a
shooter glass.

Cerebral Hemorrhage
1 oz. Kahlua
1 oz. Peach Schnapps
1 oz. Baileys Irish Cream

Layer ingredients in order
given in a shooter glass.
Slowly pour 3 drops of
Grenadine in center of drink.

Chambord Kamikaze
1 ½ oz. Skyy Vodka
1 oz. Chambord
½ oz. Triple Sec
½ oz. Lime Juice

Shake all ingredients with ice
and strain into a shooter glass.
Garnish with a wedge of lime.

Chambord Kiss
½ oz. Chambord
½ oz. Baileys Irish Cream

Layer ingredients in order
given in a shot glass.

Chambord Shooter
1 oz. Chambord
½ oz.. Vodka
½ oz. Triple Sec
1 oz. Pineapple Juice

Shake all ingredients with ice
and strain into a shooter glass.

Chantilly Lace
1 oz. Grand Marnier
1 oz. Tia Maria
½ oz. Hot Coffee

Combine all ingredients in a
shooter glass. Top with a dash
of whipped cream.

Chapped Asshole
1 ¼ oz. Jack Daniel's
1 ¼ oz. Amaretto

Stir both ingredients with ice
and strain into a shooter glass.
Float ¼ oz. Bacardi 151 Rum
on top. Ignite with a match.

Charlie Chaplin
1 oz. Sloe Gin
1 oz. Apricot Brandy
1 oz. Sour Mix

Shake all ingredients with ice
and strain into a shooter glass.

Charlie's Angel
1 ½ oz. Amaretto
½ oz. Cream

Pour amaretto into a shooter
glass and float cream on top.

Chastity Belt
1 oz. Frangelico
1 oz. Baileys Irish Cream
1 oz. Tia Maria
Dash of Cream

Layer ingredients in order
given in a shooter glass.

Cheesy Poof
2 oz. Red Wine
½ oz. Tabasco Sauce
1 tsp. Salt
1 raw Egg
1 Beef Bouillon Cube

Combine all ingredients in a
blender without ice. Process
until smooth. Pour into a
shooter glass. Top with a
sprinkle grated parmesan
cheese.

Cherry Blow Pop
¾ oz. Amaretto
¾ oz. Southern Comfort
¾ oz. Grenadine

Shake all ingredients with ice
and strain into a shooter glass.

Cherry Bomb
1 ½ oz. Bacardi 151 Rum
½ oz. Grenadine

Combine both ingredients in a
shooter glass.

Cherry Boom
3 oz. Vodka
Dash of Cranberry Juice

Chill vodka with ice and
strain into a shooter glass. Top
with a dash of cranberry juice.

Cherry Bottom
1 oz. Jack Daniel's
1 oz. Hot Damn Cinnamon
Schnapps
4 Halves of Cherries

Layer bottom of a shooter
glass with cherries. Pour in
Jack Daniel's and Hot Damn.

Cherry Chill
1 oz. Vodka
1 oz. Cherry Brandy
½ oz. Lemonade
½ oz. Pineapple Juice

Shake all ingredients with ice
and strain into a shooter glass.

Cherry Cola
1 oz. Cherry Brandy
1 oz. Captain Morgan Spiced
Rum
1 ½ oz. Cola

Shake all ingredients with ice
and strain into a shooter glass.

Cherry Cooler
1 oz. Vodka
1 oz. Cherry Brandy
½ oz. Orange Juice
½ oz. 7-Up

Shake all ingredients with ice
and strain into a shooter glass.

Cherry Cough Syrup
¾ oz. Peach Schnapps
¾ oz. Triple Sec
¾ oz. Vodka
¾ oz. Grenadine

Shake all ingredients with ice
and strain into a shooter glass.

Cherry Kamikaze
1 oz. Vodka
1 oz. Cherry Brandy
1 oz. Sour Mix

Shake all ingredients with ice
and strain into a shooter glass.

Cherry Lemondrop
1 oz. Vodka
1 oz. Cherry Brandy
1 oz. Lemonade

Shake all ingredients with ice
and strain into a shooter glass.

Cherry Lifesaver
1 oz. Cherry Brandy
¼ oz. Creme de Almond
¾ oz. Sour Mix
½ oz. 7-Up
½ oz. Grapefruit Juice

Shake all ingredients with ice
and strain into a shooter glass.

Cherry Limedrop
1 oz. Vodka
1 oz. Cherry Brandy
1 oz. Limeade

Shake all ingredients with ice
and strain into a shooter glass.

Cherry Popper
½ oz. Peach Schnapps
½ oz. Amarula Liqueur
1 Cherry

Combine all ingredients in a
shot glass.

Cherry Rum
1 ½ oz. Rum
½ oz. Cherry Brandy
1 oz. Cream

Shake all ingredients with ice
and strain into a shooter glass.

Cherry Smash
1 oz. Cherry Brandy
¾ oz. Maraschino Liqueur
¼ oz. Grenadine
¼ oz. Pineapple Juice
¾ oz. 7-Up

Shake all ingredients with ice
and strain into a shooter glass.

Cherry-O
1 ¼ oz. Kirschwasser
1 oz. Triple Sec
¼ oz. Lime Juice

Shake all ingredients with ice
and strain into a shooter glass.

Chia Pet
1 ½ oz. T.Q. Hot Schnapps
1 ½ oz. Midori Melon Liqueur

Shake both ingredients with
ice and strain into a shooter
glass.

Chick Replacement
1 ½ oz. Vodka
1 ½ oz. Chocolate Syrup

Combine both ingredients in a
shooter glass.

Chicken Fetus in a Bucket
¾ oz. White Sambuca
¼ oz. Cherry Avacarte
¼ oz. Clear Avacarte

Layer ingredients in order
given in a shooter glass.

China Mold
1 oz. Baileys Irish Cream
1 oz. Light Creme de Cacao
Dash White Creme de Menthe

Shake all ingredients with ice
and strain into a shooter glass.

China White
1 oz. Baileys Irish Cream
1 oz. Light Creme de Cacao
1 oz. Cinnamon Schnapps

Shake all ingredients with ice
and strain into a shooter glass.

Chinchilla
1 oz. Benedictine
1 oz. Triple Sec
1 oz. Cream

Shake all ingredients with ice
and strain into a shooter glass.

Chocolate Cake
¾ oz. Vodka
¾ oz. Frangelico

Shake both ingredients with
ice and strain into a shooter
glass. Serve with a sugar-
coated lemon slice.

Chocolate Chip
1 oz. Dark Creme de Cacao
1 oz. Frangelico
1 oz. Cream

Shake all ingredients with ice
and strain into a shooter glass.

Chocolate Covered Cherry
½ oz. Godiva Chocolate
Liqueur
½ oz. Amaretto di Saronno
½ oz. Baileys Irish Cream

Layer ingredients in order
given in a shooter glass.

**Chocolate Covered
Raspberry**
1 oz. Dark Creme de Cacao
¾ oz. Razzmatazz
¼ oz. Baileys Irish Cream
Splash of Cream

Shake all ingredients with ice
and strain into a shooter glass.

Chocolate Daisy
1 ½ oz. Brandy
1 ½ oz. Port Wine
1 oz. Sour Mix
Dash of Grenadine

Shake all ingredients with ice
and strain into a shooter glass.

Chocolate Jizz
1 ½ oz. Godiva White
Chocolate Liqueur
1 oz. Kahlua

Shake both ingredients with
ice and strain into a shooter
glass.

Chocolate Milk
1 oz. Baileys Irish Cream
1 oz. Godiva Chocolate
Liqueur

Shake both ingredients with
ice and strain into a shooter
glass.

Chocolate Pucker
½ oz. Absolut Vodka
½ oz. Creme de Banana
½ oz. Light Creme de Cacao
½ oz. Lemonade

Shake all ingredients with ice
and strain into a shooter glass.

Chocolate Pussy
¾ oz. Creme de Banana
¾ oz. Amaretto
¾ oz. Vodka
¾ oz. Sour Mix
½ oz. Chocolate Syrup

Shake all ingredients with ice
and strain into a shooter glass.

Chocolate Rattlesnake
¾ oz. Dark Creme de Cacao
¾ oz. Peppermint Schnapps
1 ½ oz. Baileys Irish Cream

Shake all ingredients with ice
and strain into a shooter glass.

Chocolate Rum
1 ½ oz. Light Rum
¾ oz. Light Creme de Cacao
¾ oz. White Creme de
Menthe
½ oz. Cream
¼ oz. Bacardi 151 Rum

Shake all ingredients with ice
and strain into a shooter glass.

Christmas
1 oz. Grenadine
2 oz. Green Creme de Menthe

Layer ingredients in order
given in a shooter glass.

Christmas Hug
1 oz. Cherry Brandy
1 oz. Parfait Amour
1 oz. Baileys Irish Cream

Shake all ingredients with ice
and strain into a shooter glass.

Christmas Jizz
1 oz. Egg Nog Liqueur
½ oz. Amaretto
½ oz. Kahlua

Layer ingredients in order
given in a shooter glass.

Christmas Tree
½ oz. Cherry Brandy
½ oz. Vodka
½ oz. Green Creme de
Menthe

Layer ingredients in order
given in a shooter glass.

Cinn-A-Bunn
½ oz. Hot Damn Cinnamon
Schnapps
½ oz. Frangelico
½ oz. Buttershots Schnapps
¼ oz. Baileys Irish Cream

Shake all ingredients with ice
and strain into a shooter glass.

Cinnamon Apple Pie
1 ½ oz. Apple Schnapps
½ oz. Cinnamon Schnapps

Shake both ingredients with
ice and strain into a shooter
glass.

Cinnamon Toast Crunch
1 oz. Butterscotch Schnapps
½ oz. Cinnamon Schnapps
1 oz. Baileys Irish Cream

Layer ingredients in order
given in a shooter glass.

Cinnastick
1 oz. Jägermeister
1 oz. After Shock Cinnamon
Liqueur

Layer ingredients in order
given in a shooter glass.

Citron My Face
¾ oz. Absolut Citron Vodka
¾ oz. Key Largo Schnapps
½ oz. Sour Mix
½ oz. Cranberry Juice
½ oz. Pineapple Juice

Shake all ingredients with ice
and strain into a shooter glass.

Citrus Slammer
2 oz. Fresca
Pinch of Cherry Kool-Aid
Powder
1 ½ oz. Bacardi 151 Rum

Combine Fresca and Kool-
Aid powder in a shooter glass.
Stir. Float Bacardi 151 Rum
on top.

Climax
½ oz. Light Creme de Cacao
½ oz. Amaretto
½ oz. Triple Sec
½ oz. Vodka
½ oz. Creme de Banana
1 oz. Cream

Shake all ingredients with ice
and strain into a shooter glass.

Clit Lick
1 oz. Tequila
1 oz. Orange Juice

Shake both ingredients with
ice and strain into a shooter
glass.

Cobra
¾ oz. Jägermeister
¾ oz. Rumple Minze
¾ oz. Baileys Irish Cream

Layer ingredients in order
given in a shooter glass.

Cobra Venom
1 oz. White Sambuca
1 oz. Rumple Minze

Shake both ingredients with
ice and strain into a shooter
glass.

Cocaine Fizz
1 ½ oz. Vodka
¾ oz. Peppermint Schnapps
Dash of Grenadine

Shake all ingredients with ice
and strain into a shooter glass.

Cocaine Shooter
½ oz. Vodka
½ oz. Chambord
½ oz. Southern Comfort
½ oz. Cranberry Juice
½ oz. Orange Juice

Shake all ingredients with ice
and strain into a shooter glass.

Cocksucking Cowboy
2 oz. Butterscotch Schnapps
½ oz. Baileys Irish Cream

Layer ingredients in order
given in a shooter glass.

Coconut Bon-Bon
1 ½ oz. Malibu Rum
½ oz. Amaretto
½ oz. Dark Creme de Cacao
¼ oz. Orange Juice
¼ oz. Cream

Shake all ingredients with ice
and strain into a shooter glass.

Coconut Cream Pie
1 ½ oz. Malibu Rum

Stir rum with ice and strain
into a shooter glass. Top with
whipped cream.

Coffee Bean
1 oz. Kahlua
1 oz. Anisette
1 oz. Southern Comfort

Shake all ingredients with ice
and strain into a shooter glass.

Cold Turkey
1 oz. Wild Turkey
¼ oz. Amaretto
¼ oz. Harvey's Bristol Cream
Sherry
¼ oz. 7-Up
¼ oz. Lime Juice
½ oz. Sour Mix

Shake all ingredients with ice
and strain into a shooter glass.

Colombian Necktie
1 oz. Rumple Minze
1 oz. Cinnamon Schnapps
1 oz. Bacardi 151 Rum
Dash of Tabasco Sauce

Shake all ingredients with ice
and strain into a shooter glass.

Coma
1 oz. Kahlua
1 oz. Creme de Banana
1 oz. Anisette

Shake all ingredients with ice
and strain into a shooter glass.

Come Fuck Me Harder
½ oz. Bacardi Light Rum
½ oz. Vodka
½ oz. Amaretto
½ oz. Sloe Gin
½ oz. Sunny Delight Orange
Drink

Shake all ingredients with ice
and strain into a shooter glass.

Comfort Killer
1 ¼ oz. Southern Comfort
1 oz. Grenadine
½ oz. Lemon Juice

Combine all ingredients in a
shooter glass. Top with a dash
of whipped cream.

Cookie Monster
1 ½ oz. Baileys Irish Cream
1 oz. Bacardi 151 Rum

Layer ingredients in order
given in a shooter glass.
Ignite with a match.

Cool Blues
1 ¼ oz. Blueberry Schnapps
¾ oz. White Creme de
Menthe
½ oz. Blue Curacao

Shake all ingredients with ice
and strain into a shooter glass.

Cool Cougar
1 ¼ oz. Jack Daniel's
1 ¼ oz. Peppermint Schnapps

Shake both ingredients with
ice and strain into a shooter
glass.

Cool of the Evening
1 oz. Vodka
1 oz. Peach Schnapps
½ oz. Cranberry Juice
½ oz. Pineapple Juice

Shake all ingredients with ice
and strain into a shooter glass.

Copper Camel
1 oz. Butterscotch Schnapps
1 oz. Baileys Irish Cream

Layer ingredients in order
given in a shooter glass.

Copper Cowboy
1 oz. Butterscotch Schnapps
1 oz. Kahlua

Shake both ingredients with
ice and strain into a shooter
glass.

Coppertone
1 oz. Malibu Rum
1 oz. Apple Schnapps

Shake both ingredients with
ice and strain into a shooter
glass.

Corridor on Fire
1 oz. Coffee Liqueur
1 oz. Baileys Irish Cream

Shake both ingredients with
ice and strain into a shooter
glass. Float ½ oz. cognac on
top. Ignite with a match.

Cosmos
1 ½ oz. Vodka
½ oz. Lime Juice

Shake both ingredients with
ice and strain into a shooter
glass.

Cotton Candy
1 oz. Strawberry Liqueur
1 oz. Licor 43
½ oz. Grenadine
½ oz. Pineapple Juice
½ oz. Orange Juice

Shake all ingredients with ice
and strain into a shooter glass.

Cough Drop
1 ½ oz. Peppermint Schnapps
1 ½ oz. Drambuie

Shake both ingredients with
ice and strain into a shooter
glass.

Cough Syrup
1 oz. Amaretto
1 oz. Southern Comfort
½ oz. Grenadine

Shake all ingredients with ice
and strain into a shooter glass.

Cowboy
1 oz. Rye Whiskey
1 oz. Tequila
1 oz. Drambuie

Shake all ingredients with ice
and strain into a shooter glass.

Cowboy Cocksucker
¾ oz. Vodka
¾ oz. Kahlua
¾ oz. Melon Liqueur

Shake all ingredients with ice
and strain into a shooter glass.

Crack Pipe
1 ½ oz. Goldschlager
1 ½ oz. Bacardi 151 Rum

Layer ingredients in order
given in a shooter glass.
Ignite with a match.

Cracked Earth
¾ oz. Coffee Liqueur
¾ oz. Baileys Irish Cream
¾ oz. Peppermint Schnapps

Layer ingredients in order
given in a shooter glass.

Crackhaus
1 oz. Blackhaus
½ oz. Cranberry Juice

Shake both ingredients with
ice and strain into a shooter
glass.

Cranapple
1 ½ oz. Apple Schnapps
1 ½ oz. Cranberry Juice

Shake both ingredients with
ice and strain into a shooter
glass.

Cranberry Pussy
½ oz. Peach Schnapps
½ oz. Midori Melon Liqueur
½ oz. Rum
½ oz. Razzmatazz Schnapps
Splash of 7-Up
Splash of Cranberry Juice

Shake all ingredients with ice
and strain into a shooter glass.

Crazy Nazi
1 oz. Jägermeister
1 oz. Rumple Minze

Shake both ingredients with
ice and strain into a shooter
glass.

Crazy Noggie
½ oz. Amaretto
½ oz. Light Rum
½ oz. 100 Proof Southern
Comfort
½ oz. Vodka

Shake all ingredients with ice
and strain into a shooter glass.

Cream of Melon
1 oz. Melon Liqueur
1 oz. Vodka
1 oz. Cream

Shake all ingredients with ice
and strain into a shooter glass.

Creamer
1 ¼ oz. Vodka
½ oz. French Vanilla Coffee
Creamer

Layer ingredients in order
given in a shooter glass.

Creamsicle
1 oz. Galliano
1 oz. Orange Juice
1 oz. Whipped Cream

Shake all ingredients with ice
and strain into a shooter glass.

Creamy Death
1 ¼ oz. Baileys Irish Cream
1 oz. Jägermeister

Shake both ingredients with
ice and strain into a shooter
glass.

Creamy Dream
½ oz. Baileys Irish Cream
½ oz. White Creme de
Menthe
¼ oz. Vodka
1 oz. Cream

Shake all ingredients with ice
and strain into a shooter glass.

Creamy Vacation in Malibu
1 oz. Captain Morgan Spiced
Rum
1 oz. Malibu Rum
1 oz. Baileys Irish Cream

Shake all ingredients with ice
and strain into a shooter glass.

Crem Louis
¾ oz. Light Creme de Cacao
¾ oz. Grand Marnier
¾ oz. Cointreau
¾ oz. Cream

Shake all ingredients with ice
and strain into a shooter glass.

Crema Cafe
¾ oz. White Sambuca
¾ oz. Kahlua
¾ oz. Cream

Shake all ingredients with ice
and strain into a shooter glass.

Crippler
1 oz. Bacardi 151 Rum
1 oz. Grain Alcohol
1 oz. Triple Sec

Shake all ingredients with ice
and strain into a shooter glass.

Crispy Crunch
1 ½ oz. Dark Creme de Cacao
1 ½ oz. Frangelico

Shake both ingredients with
ice and strain into a shooter
glass.

Crocket
1 ½ oz. Cheri-Beri Pucker
Schnapps
½ oz. Sour Mix
¼ oz. Grenadine

Shake all ingredients with ice
and strain into a shooter glass.

Crown Bomb
¾ oz. Crown Royal
¾ oz. Amaretto
¾ oz. Malibu Rum
¾ oz. Pineapple Juice

Shake all ingredients with ice
and strain into a shooter glass.

Cucaracha
1 oz. Tequila
½ oz. Brandy
½ oz. Coffee Creamer

Layer ingredients in order
given in a shooter glass.

Cucumber
1 oz. Green Creme de Menthe
1 oz. Cream

Shake both ingredients with
ice and strain into a shooter
glass.

Cuervo Slammer
1 oz. Cuervo Gold Tequila
½ oz. Ginger Ale

Combine both ingredients in a
large shot glass. Cover with a
bar coaster, and slam down.
Drink while fizzing.

Cum in a Hot Tub
1 oz. Vodka
½ oz. Rum

Combine both ingredients
(without chilling) in shooter
glass. Slowly add 3 drops
Baileys Irish Cream to center
of drink.

Cum Scorcher
½ oz. Butterscotch Schnapps
½ oz. Kahlua
½ oz. Vodka
¼ oz. Baileys Irish Cream

Layer ingredients in order
given in a shooter glass.

Cum Shot
½ oz. White Sambuca
½ oz. Goldschlager
½ oz. Bacardi 151 Rum

Layer ingredients in order
given in a shooter glass.
Top with a dash of whipped
cream.

Cum Stain
1 oz. Tequila
1 oz. Amaretto

Combine both ingredients in a
shooter glass. Slowly pour a
dash of Baileys Irish Cream
into the center of the drink.

Cum Too Soon
1 oz. Bourbon
1 oz. Peach Schnapps
1 oz. Vodka

Shake all ingredients with ice
and strain into a shooter glass.

Cumdrop
1 oz. Kahlua
1 oz. Baileys Irish Cream
½ oz. Creme de Banana

Shake all ingredients with ice
and strain into a shooter glass.

Cunnilingus
¼ oz. Baileys Irish Cream
¼ oz. Peach Schnapps
½ oz. Pineapple juice

Shake all ingredients with ice
and strain into a shot glass.
Top with a dash of whipped
cream.

Cyanide
1 ½ oz. Rum
¾ oz. Creme de Noyeaux
1 ½ oz. Cream

Shake all ingredients with ice
and strain into a shooter glass.

Cyclone Attack
1 ½ oz. Blue Curacao
1 ½ oz. Lemon Juice

Layer ingredients in order
given in a shooter glass.

Cyrano
1 oz. Grand Marnier
1 oz. Baileys Irish Cream
¼ oz. Chambord

Layer ingredients in order
given in a shooter glass.

Dancing Cowboy
1 oz. Creme de Banana
1 oz. Kahlua
1 oz. Baileys Irish Cream

Layer ingredients in order
given in a shooter glass.

Dark Crystal
1 oz. Vodka
¾ oz. Dark Creme de Cacao
¾ oz. Licor 43

Shake all ingredients with ice
and strain into a shooter glass.

Dawg Tail
1 oz. Gin
1 oz. Midori Melon Liqueur
1 oz. Orange Juice

Shake all ingredients with ice
and strain into a shooter glass.
Top with a dash of Grenadine.

DC-3
1 oz. Kahlua
1 oz. Anisette
1 oz. Baileys Irish Cream

Shake all ingredients with ice
and strain into a shooter glass.

Dead Chicken
2 oz. Vodka
1 raw Egg

Combine both ingredients in a
shooter glass. Top with a dash
of Tabasco Sauce and a pinch
of salt & pepper.

Dead Doctor
1 oz. Dr. McGillicuddy's
Menthomint Schnapps
1 oz. Kahlua
1 oz. Jägermeister

Shake all ingredients with ice
and strain into a shooter glass.

Dead End
½ oz. Amaretto
½ oz. Coffee Liqueur
½ oz. Grain Alcohol
½ oz. Baileys Irish Cream

Shake all ingredients with ice
and strain into a shooter glass.

Dead Mexican Goat
1 ½ oz. Cuervo Gold Tequila
¼ oz. Cream
Dash of Tabasco Sauce

Shake all ingredients with ice
and strain into a shooter glass.

Dead Nazi
1 ½ oz. Rumple Minze
1 ½ oz. Jägermeister

Shake both ingredients with
ice and strain into a shooter
glass.

Dead Nazi from Hell
¾ oz. Rumple Minze
¾ oz. Jägermeister
¾ oz. Vodka

Shake all ingredients with ice
and strain into a shooter glass.

Death Juice
1 oz. Butterscotch Schnapps
1 oz. Kahlua
½ oz. Baileys Irish Cream
½ oz. Amaretto
¼ oz. Chocolate Syrup

Shake all ingredients with ice
and strain into a shooter glass.

Death Wish
¾ oz. Rye Whiskey
¾ oz. Jägermeister
¾ oz. Rumple Minze

Shake all ingredients with ice
and strain into a shooter glass.

Decadence
¾ oz. Kahlua
¾ oz. Frangelico
¾ oz. Baileys Irish Cream

Layer ingredients in order
given in a shooter glass.

Deep Purple
1 oz. Vodka
1 oz. Maui Tropical Schnapps
½ oz. Raspberry Schnapps
½ oz. Lemonade

Shake all ingredients with ice
and strain into a shooter glass.

Deep T
1 oz. Kahlua
1 oz. Vodka
1 oz. Baileys Irish Cream

Shake all ingredients with ice
and strain into a shooter glass.

Deep Throat
1 oz. Vodka
1 oz. Kahlua
1 oz. Amaretto
¾ oz. Baileys Irish Cream

Shake all ingredients with ice
and strain into a shooter glass.
Top with whipped cream.

Devil Shooter
1 oz. Absolut Peppar Vodka
1 oz. Yellow Chartreuse

Stir both ingredients with ice
and strain into a shooter glass.

Devil's Horn
¾ oz. Cherry Advocaat
¾ oz. Strawberry Advocaat
¾ oz. Baileys Irish Cream

Layer ingredients in order
given in a shooter glass.

Devil's Mouthwash
1 oz. Black Sambuca
1 oz. Southern Comfort

Combine both ingredients in a
shooter glass.

Diablerie
¾ oz. Peach Schnapps
¾ oz. Triple Sec
¾ oz. Raspberry Schnapps
Dash of Grenadine

Shake all ingredients with ice
and strain into a shooter glass.

Dickory
¾ oz. Vodka
¾ oz. Tequila
½ oz. Apple Brandy
½ oz. Blueberry Schnapps

Shake all ingredients with ice
and strain into a shooter glass.

**Did You Get the Number of
That Truck?**
1 oz. Bourbon
1 oz. Apple Schnapps
½ oz. Cinnamon Schnapps
1 oz. Squirt Soda

Shake all ingredients with ice
and strain into a shooter glass.

Diesel
1 oz. Bacardi 151 Rum
1 oz. Firewater Cinnamon
Schnapps

Combine both ingredients in a
shooter glass.

Dimetapp
1 oz. Blue Curacao
1 oz. Grenadine

Stir both ingredients with ice
and strain into a shooter glass.

Dingbat
1 oz. Dark Rum
1 oz. Kahlua
1 oz. Cream

Shake all ingredients with ice
and strain into a shooter glass.

Dingy Scream
½ oz. Scotch
½ oz. Cola
1 oz. Lime Juice

Shake all ingredients with ice
and strain into a shooter glass.
Float 1 oz. Baileys Irish
Cream on top.

Dipsy Cruiser
1 oz. Southern Comfort
1 oz. Amaretto
½ oz. Lime Juice

Shake all ingredients with ice
and strain into a shooter glass.

Dirty Banana
1 oz. Creme de Banana
1 oz. Dark Creme de Cacao
1 oz. Cream

Shake all ingredients with ice
and strain into a shooter glass.

Dirty Bird
1 oz. Kahlua
1 oz. Wild Turkey 101
1 oz. Orange Juice

Shake all ingredients with ice
and strain into a shooter glass.

Dirty Buffalo
3 oz. Beer
1 oz. Bourbon
1 ½ oz. Cola
1 raw Egg

Shake all ingredients with ice
and strain into a shooter glass.

Dirty Dimebag
1 ½ oz. Bacardi 151 Rum
Dash of Tabasco Sauce
Pinch of Ground Black Pepper

Shake all ingredients with ice
and strain into a shooter glass.
Top with ½ teaspoon grated
parmesan cheese.

Dirty Girl Scout
1 oz. Dark Creme de Cacao
1 oz. White Creme de Menthe
1 oz. Cream

Shake all ingredients with ice
and strain into a shooter glass.

Dirty Girl Scout Cookie
1 oz. Green Creme de Menthe
1 ¼ oz. Baileys Irish Cream

Shake both ingredients with
ice and strain into a shooter
glass.

Dirty Orgasm
¾ oz. Baileys Irish Cream
¾ oz. Galliano
¾ oz. Grand Marnier

Layer ingredients in order
given in a shooter glass.

Dirty Panties
1 oz. Tequila
Pinch of Grated Parmesan
Cheese

Combine both ingredients in a
shot glass.

Dirty Sanchez
1 ½ oz. Triple Sec
1 oz. Vodka
½ oz. Lime Juice
Splash of Pink Grapefruit
Juice

Shake all ingredients with ice
and strain into a frozen
shooter glass.

Dirty White Bitch
½ oz. Kahlua
½ oz. Vodka
½ oz. Chambord
½ oz. Midori Melon Liqueur
½ oz. Pineapple Juice
½ oz. Cream

Shake all ingredients with ice
and strain into a shooter glass.

Ditch Pig
1 oz. Blue Curacao
1 oz. Frangelico

Layer ingredients in order
given in a shooter glass.

Do Me Juice
¼ oz. Cinnamon Schnapps
¼ oz. Peppermint Schnapps
¼ oz. Bacardi 151 Rum
¼ oz. Jägermeister

Shake all ingredients with ice
and strain into a shot glass.

DOA
1 oz. Parfait Amour
1 oz. Anisette
1 oz. Tequila

Shake all ingredients with ice
and strain into a shooter glass.

Doc's Booster Shot
1 oz. Dr. McGillicuddy's
Menthomint Schnapps
1 oz. Canadian Whisky

Shake both ingredients with
ice and strain into a shooter
glass.

Doc's Dog
1 ½ oz. Dr. McGillicuddy's
Menthomint Schnapps
Dash of Tabasco Sauce

Combine both ingredients in a
large shot glass.

Doc's Medicine
1 ¼ oz. Southern Comfort
1 oz. Tequila

Shake both ingredients with
ice and strain into a shooter
glass.

Domestic Quarrel
½ oz. Kahlua
½ oz. Amaretto
½ oz. Baileys Irish Cream
½ oz. Vodka
½ oz. Cream

Shake all ingredients with ice
and strain into a shooter glass.

Don Quixote
1 oz. Tequila
1 oz. Guinness Stout

Combine both ingredients in a
shooter glass.

Donkey Punch
1 ½ oz. Kahlua
1 oz. Sour Apple Pucker
Schnapps

Shake both ingredients with
ice and strain into a shooter
glass. Top with a pinch of
alfalfa sprouts.

Double Berry Blast
1 oz. Blueberry Schnapps
1 oz. Strawberry Juice

Stir both ingredients with ice
and strain into a shooter glass.

Double Gold
1 oz. Goldschlager
1 oz. Cuervo Gold Tequila

Layer ingredients in order
given in a shooter glass.

Double Mint Hit
2 oz. White Creme de Menthe
2 oz. Peppermint Schnapps
4 Altoids Mints

Crush up the mints in the
bottom of a shooter glass.
Pour in remaining ingredients.

Double Vision
¾ oz. Vodka
¾ oz. Malibu Rum
¾ oz. Hot Shot Schnapps
¼ oz. Sour Mix
Splash of Pineapple Juice
Splash of Orange Juice
Dash of Grenadine

Shake all ingredients with ice
and strain into a shooter glass.

Dr. Death
1 oz. Jack Daniel's
1 oz. Cuervo Gold Tequila
1 oz. Grand Marnier

Shake all ingredients with ice
and strain into a shooter glass.

Dr. Pepper
1 oz. Vodka
¾ oz. Amaretto
¾ oz. Cranberry Juice
Splash of Cola

Shake all ingredients with ice
and strain into a shooter glass.

Dragon Slayer
1 oz. Green Chartreuse
1 oz. Tequila

Layer ingredients in order
given in a shooter glass.

Dragoon
¾ oz. Kahlua
¾ oz. Baileys Irish Cream
¾ oz. Black Sambuca

Shake all ingredients with ice
and strain into a shooter glass.

Dreamsicle
1 oz. Vanilla Schnapps
1 oz. Orange Juice
1 oz. Cream

Layer ingredients in order
given in a shooter glass.

Drunken Sammy
½ oz. Grenadine
1 oz. Bacardi 151 Rum
½ oz. Blue Curacao

Layer ingredients in order
given in a shooter glass.

Duck Fart
1 ½ oz. Kahlua
1 ½ oz. Canadian Club

Shake both ingredients with
ice and strain into a shooter
glass.

Duck Fuck
2 oz. Tanqueray Gin
½ oz. Absolut Vodka
2 oz. Ice Beer

Combine all ingredients in a
shooter glass.

Duckpin
1 oz. Chambord
1 oz. Southern Comfort
1 oz. Pineapple Juice

Shake all ingredients with ice
and strain into a shooter glass.

Duck's Ass
¾ oz. Baileys Irish Cream
¾ oz. Kahlua
¾ oz. Bacardi 151 Rum

Shake all ingredients with ice
and strain into a shooter glass.

Dumbfuck
½ oz. Canadian Whisky
½ oz. After Shock Cinnamon
Liqueur

Combine both ingredients in a
shot glass.

Dundalk
¾ oz. Licor 43
¾ oz. Melon Liqueur
½ oz. Cream

Layer ingredients in order
given in a shooter glass.

E.T.
1 oz. Dry Gin
1 oz. After Shock Cinnamon
Liqueur

Layer ingredients in order
given in a shooter glass.

Easter Egg
¾ oz. Chambord
¾ oz. Tia Maria ¾ oz. Cream

Layer ingredients in order
given in a shooter glass.

Easy Lay
¾ oz. Baileys Irish Cream
¾ oz. Dark Creme de Cacao
¾ oz. Cream

Shake all ingredients with ice
and strain into a shooter glass.

Eclipse
1 ½ oz. Sloe Gin
1 oz. Gin
¼ oz. Grenadine

Place a cherry in the bottom
of a shooter glass; add
Grenadine. Float other
ingredients on top. Garnish
with an orange twist.

Eggnog Shooter
1 ¼ oz. Light Rum
1 raw Egg
1 tsp. Sugar
3 oz. Cream
Dash of Nutmeg

Shake all ingredients with ice
and strain into a shooter glass.

Eight Second Ride
¾ oz. Wild Turkey
¾ oz. Bacardi 151 Rum
¾ oz. Jägermeister

Shake all ingredients with ice
and strain into a shooter glass.

El Bastardo
1 oz. Everclear
1 oz. Jack Daniel's
5 Dashes Tabasco Sauce

Shake all ingredients with ice
and strain into a shooter glass.

El Chico
1 oz. Tequila
½ oz. Triple Sec
½ oz. Lime Juice
2 Dashes Bitters

Shake all ingredients with ice
and strain into a shooter glass.

El Rancho Brandy
1 ½ oz. Brandy
1 ½ oz. Bourbon
¼ oz. Grand Marnier
¼ oz. Sour Mix

Shake all ingredients with ice
and strain into a shooter glass.

Elberfelt
1 ¼ oz. Strawberry Liqueur
½ oz. Light Creme de Cacao
¼ oz. Maraschino Liqueur
¼ oz. Pineapple Juice
¾ oz. Cream

Shake all ingredients with ice
and strain into a shooter glass.

Electric Banana
1 ½ oz. Tequila
1 ½ oz. Creme de Banana

Shake both ingredients with
ice and strain into a shooter
glass.

Electric Popsicle
¾ oz. Parfait Amour
¾ oz. Vodka
¾ oz. Creme de Banana
¾ oz. Lime Juice

Shake all ingredients with ice
and strain into a shooter glass.

Electric Watermelon
1 oz. Melon Liqueur
1 oz. Vodka
½ oz. Lemonade
½ oz. Orange Juice
¼ oz. Grenadine

Shake all ingredients with ice
and strain into a shooter glass.

Electrical Storm
½ oz. Goldschlager
½ oz. Baileys Irish Cream
½ oz. Jägermeister
½ oz. Rumple Minze

Shake all ingredients with ice
and strain into a shooter glass.

Embryo
1 ½ oz. Galliano
3 drops Baileys Irish Cream

Pour Galliano into a shooter
glass. Slowly add Baileys.
Don't stir.

Endless Summer
1 oz. Tequila
½ oz. Triple Sec
Dash of Lime Juice

Shake all ingredients with ice
and strain into a large shot
glass.

Energizer
¾ oz. Benedictine
¾ oz. Baileys Irish Cream
¾ oz. Grand Marnier

Layer ingredients in order
given in a shooter glass.

Erase Your Face
½ oz. Light Rum
½ oz. Gold Rum
½ oz. Dark Rum
¼ oz. Triple Sec
1 oz. Sour Mix
1 oz. Cranberry Juice

Shake all ingredients with ice
and strain into a shooter glass.
Top with a splash of Bacardi
151 Rum.

Eskimo Kiss
¾ oz. Swiss Chocolate
Almond Liqueur
¾ oz. Cherry Brandy
¾ oz. Amaretto

Layer ingredients in order
given in a shooter glass.
Top with a dash of whipped
cream.

Eskimo Slugger
1 oz. Rumple Minze
1 oz. Baileys Irish Cream
1 oz. Butterscotch Schnapps

Shake all ingredients with ice
and strain into a shooter glass.

Evening Shade
¾ oz. Baileys Irish Cream
 ¾ oz. Buttershots Schnapps
Splash of Pineapple Juice

Shake all ingredients with ice
and strain into a shooter glass.

Evil Blue Thing
1 ½ oz. Light Creme de Cacao
1 oz. Blue Curacao
½ oz. Light Rum

Shake all ingredients with ice
and strain into a shooter glass.

Exorcist
1 ½ oz. Tequila
1 ½ oz. Peppermint Schnapps

Shake both ingredients with
ice and strain into a shooter
glass.

Exploding Cherry
1 oz. Tequila
1 oz. Maraschino Liqueur
1 oz. Sour Mix

Shake all ingredients with ice
and strain into a shooter glass.
Drop a cherry into the drink.
Top with a spoonful of Pop
Rocks candies.

Explosive Orgasm
1 oz. Creme de Banana
1 oz. Peach Schnapps

Shake both ingredients with
ice and strain into a shooter
glass.

Extra Strength Tylenol
1 oz. Gin
1 oz. Tequila
1 oz. Cream
Dash of Creme de Noyeaux

Shake all ingredients with ice
and strain into a shooter glass.

F "Un" Hot
1 ½ oz. Absolut Peppar
Vodka
1 ½ oz. Cinnamon Schnapps

Combine both ingredients in a
shooter glass.

F-16
¾ oz. Kahlua
¾ oz. Frangelico
¾ oz. Baileys Irish Cream

Layer ingredients in order
given in a shooter glass.

Fence Jumper
½ oz. Bacardi 151 Rum
½ oz. Tequila
Dash of Tabasco Sauce

Combine all ingredients in a
shot glass.

Fender Bender
1 ½ oz. Peach Schnapps
1 ½ oz. Yellow Chartreuse

Shake both ingredients with
ice and strain into a shooter
glass.

**Festering Slobovian
Hummer**
1 oz. Peppermint Schnapps
1 oz. Galliano
1 oz. Bacardi 151 Rum

Shake all ingredients with ice
and strain into a shooter glass.

Fiery Kiss
1 oz. Cinnamon Schnapps
Dash of Honey

Shake both ingredients with
ice and strain into a shot glass.

Fifth Avenue
1 oz. Dark Creme de Cacao
1 oz. Apricot Brandy
1 oz. Cream

Layer ingredients in order
given in a shooter glass.

Fifth Floor
½ oz. Vodka
½ oz. Brandy
½ oz. Cherry Brandy
½ oz. Cointreau
½ oz. Triple Sec
½ oz. Orange Juice
Dash of Grenadine

Shake all ingredients with ice
and strain into a shooter glass.

Fire Bird
1 oz. Absolut Peppar Vodka
2 oz. Cranberry Juice

Shake both ingredients with
ice and strain into a shooter
glass.

Fire Dragon
¾ oz. Tequila
¾ oz. Campari
¾ oz. Bacardi 151 Rum

Shake all ingredients with ice
and strain into a shooter glass.

Fire in the Hole
1 oz. Tequila
1 oz. Hot Damn Cinnamon
Schnapps
1 oz. Jägermeister

Shake all ingredients with ice
and strain into a shooter glass.

Fire on the Mountain
1 ½ oz. Hot Damn Cinnamon
Schnapps
1 ½ oz. Mountain Dew

Combine both ingredients in a
shooter glass.

Fireball
2 oz. Cinnamon Schnapps
2 Dashes Tabasco Sauce

Shake both ingredients with
ice and strain into a shooter
glass.

Firecracker
1 oz. Cinnamon Schnapps
1 oz. Cherry Brandy
1 oz. Cream

Shake all ingredients with ice
and strain into a shooter glass.

Fizzer
2 oz. Absolut Citron Vodka
Splash of 7-Up

Combine both ingredients in a
shooter glass. Cover glass
with a beer coaster and slam
down.

Flame Thrower
1 oz. Light Creme de Cacao
1 oz. Benedictine
1 oz. Brandy

Layer ingredients in order
given in a shooter glass.
Ignite with a match.

Flame Tower
2 oz. Bacardi 151 Rum
Splash of Orange Juice
Splash of Grenadine

Shake all ingredients with ice
and strain into a shooter glass.
Top with another ounce of
Bacardi 151 Rum and light
with a match.

Flaming Armadillo
1 oz. Amaretto
1 oz. Brandy

Stir both ingredients with ice
and strain into a shooter glass.
Float ½ oz. Bacardi 151 Rum
on top. Ignite with a match.

Flaming Asshole
¾ oz. Brandy
¾ oz. Light Rum
¾ oz. Tequila

Shake all ingredients with ice
and strain into a shooter glass.

Flaming B-52
1 oz. Tia Maria
1 oz. Baileys Irish Cream
1 oz. Cointreau

Layer ingredients in order
given in a shooter glass.
Ignite with a match.

Flaming Blow Job
1 oz. Jack Daniel's
1 oz. Chocolate Milk
½ oz. Grain Alcohol

Layer ingredients in order
given in a shooter glass.
Top with a dash of whipped
cream. Ignite with a match.

Flaming Blue Fuck
½ oz. Blue Curacao
1 ½ oz. White Sambuca

Layer ingredients in order
given in a shooter glass.
Ignite with a match.

Flaming Blue Steel
1 oz. Vodka
½ oz. Blue Curacao
½ oz. Peppermint Schnapps

Shake all ingredients with ice
and strain into a shooter glass.
Top with 1 oz. of Bacardi 151
Rum and light with a match.

Flaming Bob Marley
¼ oz. Grenadine
2 oz. Green Creme de Menthe
½ oz. 190 Proof Grain
Alcohol

Layer ingredients in order
given in a shooter glass.
Ignite with a match.

Flaming Brass
1 ½ oz. Goldschlager
½ oz. After Shock Cinnamon
Liqueur

Layer ingredients in order
given in a shooter glass.
Ignite with a match.

Flaming Cockroach
1 oz. Kahlua
1 oz. Bacardi 151 Rum
1 oz. Tequila

Layer ingredients in order
given in a shooter glass.
Ignite with a match.

Flaming Code
1 oz. After Shock Cinnamon
Liqueur
1 oz. Vodka
1 oz. Bacardi 151 Rum

Layer ingredients in order
given in a shooter glass.
Ignite with a match.

Flaming Dead Nazi
¾ oz. Jägermeister
¾ oz. Goldschlager
¾ oz. Bacardi 151 Rum

Layer ingredients in order
given in a shooter glass.
Ignite with a match.

Flaming Dragon Snot
1 oz. Green Creme de Menthe
Dash of Baileys Irish Cream
Dash of Bacardi 151 Rum

Layer ingredients in order
given in a shot glass. Ignite
with a match.

Flaming Fart
1 ½ oz. Cinnamon Schnapps
1 oz. Bacardi 151 Rum

Layer ingredients in order
given in a shooter glass.
Ignite with a match.

Flaming Fireman
1 oz. Goldschlager
1 oz. Triple Sec
1 oz. Bacardi 151 Rum

Combine all ingredients in a
shooter glass. Ignite.

Flaming Glacier
¾ oz. After Shock Cinnamon
Liqueur
¼ oz. Rumple Minze

Layer ingredients in order
given in a shot glass. Ignite
with a match.

Flaming Harbor Light
½ oz. Kahlua
½ oz. Tequila
½ oz. Bacardi 151 Rum

Layer ingredients in order
given in a large shot glass.
Light with a match.

Flaming Jesus
1 ½ oz. Vodka
Dash of Lime Juice
Dash of Grenadine
½ oz. Bacardi 151 Rum

Combine all ingredients in a
shooter glass. Ignite with a
match.

Flaming Lemon Drop
2 oz. Absolut Citron Vodka
½ oz. Galliano

Stir both ingredients with ice
and strain into a shooter glass.
Soak a slice of lemon in some
Bacardi 151 Rum, then dip
into sugar. Place the coated
lemon slice on the shooter
glass and ignite with match.

Flaming Nazi
1 oz. Jägermeister
1 oz. Rumple Minze

Stir both ingredients with ice
and strain into a shooter glass.

Flaming Pisser
2 oz. Bacardi 151 Rum
¼ oz. Lime Juice
¾ oz. 7-Up

Combine all ingredients in a
shooter glass. Ignite with a
match.

Flaming Pumpkin Pie
¾ oz. Kahlua
¾ oz. Baileys Irish Cream
¾ oz. Goldschlager

Layer ingredients in order
given in a shooter glass.
Ignite with a match and
sprinkle a pinch of ground
cinnamon on top.

Flaming Scotsman
½ oz. Melon Liqueur
½ oz. Malibu Rum
½ oz. Chambord
¼ oz. Sour Mix

Shake all ingredients with ice
and strain into a shooter glass.

Flaming Squeegee
½ oz. Captain Morgan Spiced
Rum
½ oz. Vodka
½ oz. Orange Juice
½ oz. Lemon Juice
¾ oz. Limeade

Shake all ingredients with ice
and strain into a shooter glass.

Flaming Toad
1 oz. Bacardi 151 Rum
1 oz. Pickle Juice

Pour rum into a shooter glass.
Ignite with a match, then pour
in pickle juice.

Flaming Viking
1 oz. Bacardi 151 Rum
1 oz. Fire & Ice

Pour rum into a sugar-rimmed
shooter glass. Ignite with a
match, then pour in Fire &
Ice.

Flamingo Road
1 ½ oz. Gin
1 oz. Apricot Brandy
½ oz. Lime Juice
Dash of Grenadine

Shake all ingredients with ice
and strain into a shooter glass.

Flanders
1 oz. Sour Apple Pucker
Schnapps
1 oz. Vodka

Shake both ingredients with
ice and strain into a shooter
glass.

Flashover
¾ oz. Absolut Peppar Vodka
¼ oz. Tabasco Sauce

Combine both ingredients in a
shot glass.

Flatliner
¾ oz. White Sambuca
5 Drops Tabasco Sauce
¾ oz. White Tequila

Layer ingredients in order
given in a shooter glass.

Florida Cactus
1 oz. Tequila
1 oz. Triple Sec
½ oz. Lime Juice

Shake all ingredients with ice
and strain into a shooter glass.

Florida Joy
1 oz. Absolut Citron Vodka
½ oz. Triple Sec
1 ½ oz. Grapefruit Juice

Shake all ingredients with ice
and strain into a shooter glass.

Flukeman
1 oz. Midori Melon Liqueur
1 oz. Baileys Irish Cream

Layer ingredients in order
given in a shooter glass.

Flying Fuck
1 ½ oz. White Sambuca
1 ½ oz. Jack Daniel's

Shake both ingredients with
ice and strain into a shooter
glass.

Flying Grasshopper
1 oz. Green Creme de Menthe
1 oz. Light Creme de Cacao
1 oz. Vodka

Shake all ingredients with ice
and strain into a shooter glass.

Forehead
1 oz. Coffee Liqueur
1 oz. Baileys Irish Cream
1 oz. Chilled Water

Layer ingredients in order
given in a shooter glass.

Four Fools
½ oz. Jägermeister
½ oz. Goldschlager
½ oz. Rumple Minze
½ oz. Bacardi 151 Rum

Layer ingredients in order
given in a shooter glass.

Four Horsemen
¾ oz. Cuervo Gold Tequila
¾ oz. Jack Daniel's
¾ oz. Jim Beam
¾ oz. Johnny Walker Red

Stir all ingredients with ice
and strain into a shooter glass.

Four Leaf Clover
¾ oz. Green Creme de
Menthe
½ oz. Light Creme de Cacao
½ oz. Baileys Irish Cream
½ oz. Irish Whiskey

Layer ingredients in order
given in a shooter glass.

Fourth of July
1 oz. Grenadine
1 oz. Vodka
1 oz. Blue Curacao

Layer ingredients in order
given in a shooter glass.

Fox Fire
½ oz. Vodka
½ oz. Southern Comfort
½ oz. Blackberry Brandy
1 oz. Lemon Juice
1 oz. Orange Juice
½ oz. Simple Syrup

Shake all ingredients with ice
and strain into a shooter glass.

Fox Trot
1 oz. Kahlua
1 oz. Baileys Irish Cream
1 oz. Tequila

Shake all ingredients with ice
and strain into a shooter glass.

Fransisca
1 ½ oz. Vodka
1 tbs. Mustard

Stir both ingredients in a
shooter glass.

Freddy Kruger
¾ oz. White Sambuca
¾ oz. Vodka
¾ oz. Jägermeister

Shake all ingredients with ice
and strain into a shooter glass.

Freight Train
1 ½ oz. Jack Daniel's
½ oz. Peppermint Schnapps

Stir both ingredients with ice
and strain into a shooter glass.

French Blow Job
½ oz. Vodka
½ oz. Amaretto
½ oz. Chambord
2 oz. Cream

Shake all ingredients with ice
and strain into a shooter glass.
Top with a dash of whipped
cream.

French Canadian
¾ oz. Kahlua
¾ oz. Cointreau
¾ oz. Yukon Jack

Layer ingredients in order
given in a shooter glass.

French Kamikaze
¾ oz. Vodka
¾ oz. Triple Sec
¾ oz. Chambord
1 oz. Sour Mix

Shake all ingredients with ice
and strain into a shooter glass.

French Martini
1/3 oz. Vodka
1/3 oz. Chambord
1/3 oz. Peach Schnapps

Shake all ingredients with ice
and strain into a shot glass.

French Toast
1 oz. Goldschlager
1 oz. Baileys Irish Cream

Layer ingredients in order
given in a shooter glass.

Friday Night Special
1 oz. Southern Comfort
1 oz. Midori Melon Liqueur
½ oz. Vodka
¼ oz. Sour Mix
Splash of 7-Up

Shake all ingredients with ice
and strain into a shooter glass.

Frog's Butt
½ oz. Green Creme de
Menthe
½ oz. Light Creme de Cacao
½ oz. Baileys Irish Cream

Layer ingredients in order
given in a shooter glass.

From Russia With Love
1 ½ oz. Vodka
Dash of Lime Juice
Dash of Vinegar

Combine all ingredients in a
shooter glass.

Frosty Bitch
¾ oz. Light Creme de Cacao
¾ oz. Blue Curacao
1 ½ oz. Peach Schnapps

Shake all ingredients with ice
and strain into a shooter glass.

Frosty Death
1 ½ oz. Avalanche Blue
Peppermint Schnapps
1 oz. Black Death Vodka

Shake both ingredients with
ice and strain into a shooter
glass.

Frosty Orange
1 oz. Licor 43
1 oz. Orange Juice
½ oz. Cream

Shake all ingredients with ice
and strain into a shooter glass.

Frozen Purple Balls
1 ½ oz. Watermelon Schnapps
½ oz. Blue Curacao

Combine both ingredients in a
blender with a scoop of ice.
Process until smooth.
Serve in a shooter glass.

Fruit Basket
1 oz. Creme de Banana
1 oz. Apricot Brandy
1 oz. Baileys Irish Cream

Shake all ingredients with ice
and strain into a shooter glass.

Fruit Salad Summer
½ oz. Cheri-Beri Pucker
Schnapps
½ oz. Grape Pucker Schnapps
½ oz. Peach Schnapps
Splash of Orange Juice

Shake all ingredients with ice
and strain into a shooter glass.

Fruity Delight
¾ oz. Strawberry Schnapps
¾ oz. Blueberry Schnapps
¾ oz. Raspberry Schnapps
¾ oz. Wildberry Schnapps

Shake all ingredients with ice
and strain into a shooter glass.

Fruity Pebbles
1 oz. Absolut Citron Vodka
½ oz. Triple Sec
½ oz. Grenadine

Shake all ingredients with ice
and strain into a shooter glass.

Frumunda Balls
1 oz. Midori Melon Liqueur
½ oz. Vodka
½ oz. Pineapple Juice
1 oz. Cream
Splash of Orange Juice

Shake all ingredients with ice
and strain into a shooter glass.

Fub Duck
1 oz. Yukon Jack
1 oz. Amaretto
1 oz. Orange Juice

Shake all ingredients with ice
and strain into a shooter glass.

Fuck in the Graveyard
½ oz. Apple Schnapps
½ oz. Blue Curacao
½ oz. Rum
½ oz. Vodka
½ oz. Blueberry Schnapps
½ oz. Chambord
Splash of Orange Juice
Splash of Cranberry Juice

Shake all ingredients with ice
and strain into a shooter glass.

Fuck Jim
½ oz. Jim Beam
1 ½ oz. Sour Apple Pucker
Schnapps

Layer ingredients in order
given in a shooter glass.

Fuck Me Like a Beast
½ oz. Tequila
½ oz. Chambord
½ oz. Midori Melon Liqueur
½ oz. Orange Juice
½ oz. Pineapple Juice
Dash of Grenadine

Shake all ingredients with ice
and strain into a shooter glass.
Float ¼ oz. Bacardi 151 Rum
on top.

Fuck Me Up
¾ oz. Creme de Banana
¾ oz. Coffee Liqueur
¾ oz. Baileys Irish Cream

Shake all ingredients with ice
and strain into a shooter glass.

Fuck Me Ups
¾ oz. Southern Comfort
¾ oz. Myer's Dark Rum
¾ oz. Pineapple Juice
¾ oz. Orange Juice
¼ oz. Grenadine

Shake all ingredients with ice
and strain into a shooter glass.

Fuck You
½ oz. Rum
½ oz. Tequila
½ oz. Blueberry Schnapps
½ oz. Goldschlager
½ oz. Jack Daniel's
½ oz. Wild Turkey

Shake all ingredients with ice
and strain into a shooter glass.

Fuckin' Willie
1 ½ oz. Vodka
¾ oz. Triple Sec
¼ oz. Lime Juice
¼ oz. Amaretto

Shake all ingredients with ice
and strain into a shooter glass.

Full Body Massage
1 ½ oz. Tequila
½ oz. Triple Sec
Splash of Cranberry Juice

Shake all ingredients with ice
and strain into a shooter glass.

Funky Chicken
1 oz. Wild Turkey
1 oz. Tequila
1 oz. Bacardi 151 Rum

Combine all ingredients in a
shooter glass. Light with a
match.

Fuzz Buster
1 oz. Peach Schnapps
1 oz. Vodka
1 oz. Wildberry Schnapps
½ oz. Orange Juice

Shake all ingredients with ice
and strain into a shooter glass.

Fuzzy Ass
1 oz. Vodka
½ oz. Triple Sec
¾ oz. Peach Schnapps
½ oz. Sour Mix
Dash of Grenadine
Splash of 7-Up

Shake all ingredients with ice
and strain into a shooter glass.

Fuzzy Bastard
1 oz. Cuervo Gold Tequila
1 Altoid Peppermint

Put the peppermint in the
bottom of a shot glass. Fill
with tequila.

Fuzzy Butt Humper
1 oz. Vodka
1 ½ oz. Peach Schnapps
¼ oz. Triple Sec
½ of a Large Marshmallow

Place marshmallow half in the
bottom of a shooter glass.
Pour in remaining ingredients.
Let marshmallow dissolve
before drinking.

Fuzzy Fuck
½ oz. Jägermeister
1 oz. Peach Schnapps
1 ½ oz. Cranberry Juice

Shake all ingredients with ice
and strain into a shooter glass.

Fuzzy Mexican
1 ¼ oz. Peach Schnapps
1 ¼ oz. Tequila

Shake both ingredients with
ice and strain into a shooter
glass.

Fuzzy Mother
1 ½ oz. Gold Tequila
½ oz. Bacardi 151 Rum

Layer ingredients in order
given in a shooter glass.
Ignite with a match.

Fuzzy Nut
1 ½ oz. Peach Schnapps
1 ½ oz. Malibu Rum

Shake both ingredients with
ice and strain into a shooter
glass.

Fuzzy Nutted Banana
½ oz. Amaretto
½ oz. 99 Bananas
½ oz. Peach Schnapps
1 oz. Orange Juice
Dash of Grenadine

Shake all ingredients with ice
and strain into a shooter glass.

Fuzzy Piss Bomb
1 oz. Peach Schnapps
1 oz. Mountain Dew

Combine both ingredients in a
shooter glass.

Galactic Ale
1 oz. Vodka
1 oz. Blue Curacao
¾ oz. Lime Juice
½ oz. Black Raspberry
Liqueur

Shake all ingredients with ice
and strain into a shooter glass.

Galliano Liquore
1 oz. Coffee Liqueur
1 oz. Galliano
½ oz. Cream

Layer ingredients in order
given in a shooter glass.

Gambler
1 oz. Tequila
1 oz. Red Wine
1 oz. Cola
Pinch of Salt

Combine all ingredients in a
shooter glass.

Gandy Dancer
¾ oz. Yukon Jack
¾ oz. Amaretto
¾ oz. Creme de Banana
¾ oz. Pineapple Juice

Shake all ingredients with ice
and strain into a shooter glass.

Garbage Can Shooter
½ oz. Amaretto
½ oz. Southern Comfort
½ oz. Triple Sec
½ oz. Licor 43
½ oz. Vodka
½ oz. Orange Juice
½ oz. Cranberry Juice

Shake all ingredients with ice
and strain into a shooter glass.

Garbaldi
1 oz. Galliano
½ oz. Amaretto
½ oz. Cream
1 oz. Orange Juice

Shake all ingredients with ice
and strain into a shooter glass.

Garden of Eden
1 oz. Absolut Mandarin
Vodka
1 oz. Peach Schnapps
½ oz. Orange Juice
½ oz. 7-Up

Shake all ingredients with ice
and strain into a shooter glass.

Gasoline Shot
½ oz. Baileys Irish Cream
½ oz. Cola
½ oz. Vodka
½ oz. Rum
Dash of Lemon Juice

Layer ingredients in order
given in a shooter glass.

Gatorader
1 oz. Creme de Banana
1 oz. Strawberry Liqueur
1 oz. Cherry Brandy

Shake all ingredients with ice
and strain into a shooter glass.

Gay Russian
1 ½ oz. Vodka
1 ½ oz. Peach Schnapps

Shake both ingredients with
ice and strain into a shooter
glass.

Geiger Counter
½ oz. Jägermeister
½ oz. Bacardi 151 Rum

Combine both ingredients in a
shot glass. Ignite with a
match.

German Blowjob
¾ oz. Baileys Irish Cream
¾ oz. Jägermeister
¾ oz. Rumple Minze

Layer ingredients in order
given in a shooter glass.

German Burrito
1 oz. Jägermeister
1 oz. Tequila

Combine both ingredients in a
shooter glass.

German Cake
½ oz. Frangelico
½ oz. Kahlua
½ oz. Baileys Irish Cream
½ oz. Malibu Rum
1 oz. Cream

Shake all ingredients with ice
and strain into a shooter glass.

German Death
1 oz. Jägermeister
1 oz. Goldschlager

Shake both ingredients with
ice and strain into a shooter
glass.

German Fruit Cup
1 oz. Honey
½ oz. Grenadine
½ oz. Blue Curacao
1 oz. Black Haus Blackberry
Brandy
½ oz. Bacardi Limon Rum

Layer ingredients in order
given in a shooter glass.

Gestapo
1 oz. Jägermeister
1 oz. Rumple Minze

Shake both ingredients with
ice and strain into a shooter
glass.

Getaway Car
1 oz. Peach Schnapps
1 oz. Absolut Citron Vodka

Shake both ingredients with
ice and strain into a shooter
glass.

Ghostbuster
1 ½ oz. Peach Schnapps
½ oz. Vodka
1 oz. Cream

Shake all ingredients with ice
and strain into a shooter glass.

Gila Slammer
1 oz. Malibu Rum
1 oz. Grain Alcohol
½ oz. Melon Liqueur
½ oz. Orange Juice
½ oz. Sour Mix

Shake all ingredients with ice
and strain into a shooter glass.

Gilligan's Island
1 oz. Peach Schnapps
2 oz. Orange Juice
2 oz. Cranberry Juice

Shake all ingredients with ice
and strain into a shooter glass.

Gin & Bear It
1 oz. Gin
½ oz. Beer

Combine both ingredients in a
shooter glass.

Ginger Bread Man
½ oz. Buttershots Schnapps
½ oz. Baileys Irish Cream
½ oz. Jägermeister
½ oz. Goldschlager

Shake all ingredients with ice
and strain into a shooter glass.

Girl Scout Cookie
1 ½ oz. Tia Maria
1 ½ oz. Peppermint Schnapps

Shake both ingredients with
ice and strain into a shooter
glass.

Go Juice
1 oz. Malibu Rum
1 oz. Absolut Vodka
1 oz. Pineapple Juice

Shake all ingredients with ice
and strain into a shooter glass.

Goddamnit
1 ½ oz. Kahlua
1 oz. White Sambuca

Shake both ingredients with
ice and strain into a shooter
glass.

Godfather from Hell
1 oz. Goldschlager
1 oz. Jägermeister
1 oz. Bacardi 151 Rum

Shake all ingredients with ice
and strain into a shooter glass.

Godzilla
½ oz. Bacardi 151 Rum
½ oz. Midori Melon Liqueur
½ oz. Sour Mix
½ oz. 7-Up

Shake all ingredients with ice
and strain into a shooter glass.

Goin' South
1 oz. Yukon Jack
1 oz. Southern Comfort
1 oz. Orange Juice

Shake all ingredients with ice
and strain into a shooter glass.

Gold Furnace
1 oz. Cinnamon Schnapps
3 Dashes Tabasco Sauce

Combine both ingredients in a
shot glass.

Gold Rush
¾ oz. Chambord
¾ oz. Baileys Irish Cream
¾ oz. Goldschlager

Layer ingredients in order
given in a shooter glass.

Goldberg
1 ½ oz. Goldschlager
1 ½ oz. Avalanche Blue
Peppermint Schnapps

Shake both ingredients with
ice and strain into a shooter
glass.

Golden Cherry
1 oz. Cinnamon Schnapps
1 oz. Bacardi 151 Rum

Combine both ingredients in a
shooter glass. Top with a
splash of Grenadine. Drop a
cherry into the drink.

Golden Dream
1 oz. Tia Maria
1 oz. Galliano

Layer ingredients in order
given in a shooter glass.

Golden Jew
½ oz. Goldschlager
½ oz. Gin
½ oz. Vodka
½ oz. Bacardi Limon Rum
½ oz. Tequila

Shake all ingredients with ice
and strain into a shooter glass.

Golden Nog
1 ¼ oz. Creme de Banana
4 oz. Orange Juice
2 oz. Vanilla Yogurt
1 tsp. Honey

Shake all ingredients with ice
and strain into a shooter glass.

Golden Rose
½ oz. Goldschlager
½ oz. Tequila Rose

Combine both ingredients in a
shot glass.

Golden Russian
1 oz. Kahlua
1 oz. Amaretto
1 oz. Cream

Shake all ingredients with ice
and strain into a shooter glass.

Golden Turkey
1 oz. Goldschlager
1 oz. Wild Turkey

Combine both ingredients in a
shooter glass.

Golden Volcano
¾ oz. Goldschlager
¼ oz. Tabasco Sauce

Combine both ingredients in a
shot glass.

Goldfinger
1 oz. Goldschlager
1 oz. Amaretto
1 oz. Lemonade

Shake all ingredients with ice
and strain into a shooter glass.

Goldfish
2 oz. Vodka
1 oz. Orange Juice

Shake both ingredients with
ice and strain into a shooter
glass.

Goldschlager Chill
1 oz. Goldschlager
1 oz. Lemonade
1 oz. Pineapple Juice

Shake all ingredients with ice
and strain into a shooter glass.

Goldschlager Kamikaze
1 oz. Goldschlager
1 oz. Vodka
1 oz. Sour Mix

Shake all ingredients with ice
and strain into a shooter glass.

Goldschlager Lemondrop
1 oz. Goldschlager
2 oz. Lemonade

Shake both ingredients with
ice and strain into a shooter
glass.

Goldschlager Limedrop
1 oz. Goldschlager
2 oz. Limeade

Shake both ingredients with
ice and strain into a shooter
glass.

Good & Plenty
1 oz. Anisette
1 oz. White Sambuca

Stir both ingredients with ice
and strain into a shooter glass.

Good Liquid Cocaine
¾ oz. Amaretto
¾ oz. Southern Comfort
¾ oz. Pineapple Juice
¾ oz. Sour Mix

Shake all ingredients with ice
and strain into a shooter glass.

Good Morning Shooter
1 ¼ oz. Vodka
1 raw Egg
1 pinch Salt

Combine all ingredients in a
coffee cup.

Gorilla Breath
1 ½ oz. Vodka
½ oz. Kahlua
½ oz. Tequila
Dash of Tabasco Sauce

Shake all ingredients with ice
and strain into a shooter glass.

Gorilla Fart
1 oz. Bacardi 151 Rum
1 oz. Wild Turkey
1 oz. Ouzo

Shake all ingredients with ice
and strain into a shooter glass.

Gorilla Snot
1 oz. Baileys Irish Cream
1 oz. Port Wine

Stir both ingredients in a
shooter glass.

Grand Am
1 oz. Grand Marnier
1 oz. Amaretto

Stir both ingredients with ice
and strain into a shooter glass.

Grand Slam
½ oz. Chambord
½ oz. Absolut Vodka
1 oz. Grand Marnier

Shake all ingredients with ice
and strain into a shooter glass.

Grandma's Candy
¾ oz. White Sambuca
¼ oz. Blue Curacao

Combine both ingredients in a
shot glass.

Grape Chill
1 oz. Vodka
1 oz. Grape Schnapps
½ oz. Lemonade
½ oz. Pineapple Juice

Shake all ingredients with ice
and strain into a shooter glass.

Grape Cooler
1 oz. Vodka
1 oz. Grape Schnapps
½ oz. Orange Juice
½ oz. 7-Up

Shake all ingredients with ice
and strain into a shooter glass.

Grape Kamikaze
1 oz. Vodka
1 oz. Grape Schnapps
1 oz. Sour Mix

Shake all ingredients with ice
and strain into a shooter glass.

Grape Kool-Aid
½ oz. Blue Curacao
½ oz. Chambord
½ oz. Southern Comfort
½ oz. Pineapple Juice
½ oz. Sour Mix
1 oz. Cranberry Juice

Shake all ingredients with ice
and strain into a shooter glass.

Grape Lemondrop
1 oz. Vodka
1 oz. Grape Schnapps
1 oz. Lemonade

Shake all ingredients with ice
and strain into a shooter glass.

Grape Limedrop
1 oz. Vodka
1 oz. Grape Schnapps
1 oz. Limeade

Shake all ingredients with ice
and strain into a shooter glass.

Grape Smash
1 oz. Chambord
1 oz. Vodka
1 oz. Sour Mix
1 oz. 7-Up

Shake all ingredients with ice
and strain into a shooter glass.

Grape Sourball
1 oz. Vodka
1 oz. Grape Juice
½ oz. Lemonade
½ oz. Orange Juice

Shake all ingredients with ice
and strain into a shooter glass.

Grass Skirt
¾ oz. Absolut Mandarin
Vodka
¾ oz. Malibu Rum
½ oz. Midori Melon Liqueur
¼ oz. Pineapple Juice

Shake all ingredients with ice
and strain into a shooter glass.

Grave Digger
1 oz. Jägermeister
1 oz. Rumple Minze
1 oz. Tequila

Shake all ingredients with ice
and strain into a shooter glass.

Graveyard
¼ oz. Any ten liquors or
liqueurs

Shake all ingredients with ice
and strain into a shooter glass.

Great Balls of Fire
1 oz. Goldschlager
½ oz. Hot Damn Cinnamon
Schnapps
½ oz. After Shock Cinnamon
Liqueur

Shake all ingredients with ice
and strain into a shooter glass.

Great Scott
1 oz. Frangelico
1 oz. Amaretto
¼ oz. Bacardi 151 Rum

Layer ingredients in order
given in a shooter glass.

Great Snot
1 oz. Frangelico
1 oz. Light Creme de Cacao
¼ oz. Bacardi 151 Rum

Layer ingredients in order
given in a shooter glass.
Top with a drop of Baileys
Irish Cream.

Green Apple
1 oz. Melon Liqueur
1 oz. Apple Schnapps
Splash of 7-Up

Shake all ingredients with ice
and strain into a shooter glass.

Green Aruba
½ oz. Blue Curacao
½ oz. Gin
½ oz. Scotch
1 oz. Orange Juice

Shake all ingredients with ice
and strain into a shooter glass.
Top with 1 teaspoon crushed
ice.

Green Caribbean
1 ½ oz. Midori Melon Liqueur
1 ½ oz. Captain Morgan
Parrot Bay Rum

Shake both ingredients with
ice and strain into a shooter
glass.

Green Cockroach
1 ¼ oz. Tequila
¾ oz. Midori Melon Liqueur

Shake both ingredients with ice and strain into a shooter glass.

Green Demon
¾ oz. Vodka
¾ oz. Rum
¾ oz. Melon Liqueur
¾ oz. Lemonade

Shake all ingredients with ice and strain into a shooter glass.

Green Goddess
1 oz. Melon Liqueur
1 oz. Rum
1 oz. Pineapple Juice

Shake all ingredients with ice and strain into a shooter glass.

Green Hand Grenade
½ oz. Green Creme de Menthe
½ oz. Baileys Irish Cream
½ oz. Kahlua
½ oz. Jack Daniel's

Shake all ingredients with ice and strain into a shooter glass.

Green Hornet
1 oz. Green Creme de Menthe
1 oz. Vodka
1 oz. Cream

Shake all ingredients with ice and strain into a shooter glass.

Green Lizard
1 oz. Green Chartreuse
½ oz. Bacardi 151 Rum

Shake both ingredients with ice and strain into a shooter glass.

Green Meenie
½ oz. Goldschlager
½ oz. Bacardi 151 Rum
1 oz. Vodka
1 oz. Melon Liqueur

Shake all ingredients with ice and strain into a shooter glass.

Green Pontiac
¾ oz. Green Creme de Menthe
¾ oz. Peppermint Schnapps
¾ oz. Baileys Irish Cream

Layer ingredients in order given in a shooter glass.

Grey Matter Scatter
1 ¼ oz. Light Creme de Cacao
1 ¼ oz. Ouzo

Shake both ingredients with ice and strain into a shooter glass.

Gross One
½ oz. Amaretto
½ oz. Gin
½ oz. Jack Daniel's
½ oz. White Sambuca
½ oz. Vodka

Shake all ingredients with ice and strain into a shooter glass.

G-Spot
¾ oz. Captain Morgan Spiced Rum
¾ oz. Wilderberry Schnapps
¾ oz. Sour Mix
¾ oz. 7-Up

Shake all ingredients with ice and strain into a shooter glass.

Guam Bomb
1 oz. Kahlua
1 oz. Tequila
1 oz. Vodka

Shake all ingredients with ice and strain into a shooter glass.

Guts
1 ½ oz. Sloe Gin
½ oz. Baileys Irish Cream

Layer ingredients in order given in a shooter glass.

Hair Raiser
1/3 oz. Anisette
1/3 oz. Brandy
1/3 oz. Triple Sec

Combine all ingredients in a shot glass.

Hairy Alligator
½ oz. Bacardi 151 Rum
½ oz. Tequila

Combine both ingredients in a shot glass.

Hammer of the Gods
1 oz. Amaretto
1 oz. White Sambuca
1 oz. Southern Comfort

Shake all ingredients with ice
and strain into a shooter glass.

Hand Grenade
1 oz. Peach Schnapps
¼ oz. Club Soda
¾ oz. Bacardi 151 Rum

Layer ingredients in order
given in a shooter glass.
Light with a match.

Hangin' on a Stick
½ oz. Cuervo Gold Tequila
½ oz. Grand Marnier
½ oz. Cointreau
1 oz. Orange Juice
¼ oz. Cranberry Juice
¼ oz. Pineapple Juice

Shake all ingredients with ice
and strain into a shooter glass
with a half-salted rim.

Happy Apple
1 oz. Apple Schnapps
1 oz. Brandy
½ oz. Amaretto

Shake all ingredients with ice
and strain into a shooter glass.

Happy Hooker
½ oz. Tia Maria
½ oz. Drambuie
½ oz. Grand Marnier

Stir all ingredients with ice
and strain into a shooter glass.

Happy Rancher
½ oz. Peach Schnapps
½ oz. Vodka
½ oz. Scotch
½ oz. Melon Liqueur
½ oz. 7-Up

Shake all ingredients with ice
and strain into a shooter glass.

Harbor Light
1 oz. Green Creme de Menthe
1 oz. Strawberry Liqueur
1 oz. Cointreau

Shake all ingredients with ice
and strain into a shooter glass.

Harley Davidson
¾ oz. Midori Melon Liqueur
¾ oz. Baileys Irish Cream
¾ oz. Jägermeister

Layer ingredients in order
given in a shooter glass.

Harry Houdini
1 oz. Creme de Banana
½ oz. Amaretto
½ oz. Light Creme de Cacao
½ oz. Pineapple Juice
½ oz. Cream

Shake all ingredients with ice
and strain into a shooter glass.

Harvey Bowel Banger
1 ½ oz. Vodka
1 ½ oz. Prune Juice

Shake both ingredients with
ice and strain into a shooter
glass.

Hawaiian Punch
½ oz. Amaretto
½ oz. Southern Comfort
½ oz. Pineapple Juice
½ oz. Orange Juice
½ oz. Grenadine

Shake all ingredients with ice
and strain into a shooter glass.

Hawoo-Woo
1 oz. Vodka
½ oz. Peach Schnapps
½ oz. Cranberry Juice
½ oz. Pineapple Juice

Shake all ingredients with ice
and strain into a shooter glass.

Hazelnut Chill
1 oz. Vodka
1 oz. Frangelico
½ oz. Lemonade
½ oz. Pineapple Juice

Shake all ingredients with ice
and strain into a shooter glass.

Hazelnut Cooler
1 oz. Frangelico
1 oz. Orange Juice
1 oz. 7-Up

Shake all ingredients with ice
and strain into a shooter glass.

Hazelnut Kamikaze
1 oz. Frangelico
1 oz. Vodka
1 oz. Sour Mix

Shake all ingredients with ice
and strain into a shooter glass.

Hazelnut Lemondrop
1 oz. Frangelico
2 oz. Lemonade

Shake both ingredients with
ice and strain into a shooter
glass.

Hazelnut Limedrop
1 oz. Frangelico
2 oz. Limeade

Shake both ingredients with
ice and strain into a shooter
glass.

Hazelnut Sourball
1 oz. Frangelico
1 oz. Lemonade
1 oz. Orange Juice

Shake all ingredients with ice
and strain into a shooter glass.

Head Banger
1 oz. Ouzo
1 oz. Bacardi 151 Rum
Dash of Grenadine

Shake all ingredients with ice
and strain into a shooter glass.

Head Room
½ oz. Creme de Banana
½ oz. Midori Melon Liqueur
1 oz. Baileys Irish Cream

Layer ingredients in order
given in a shooter glass.

Hedgehopper
¾ oz. Vodka
¾ oz. Gin
¾ oz. Tequila
¼ oz. 7-Up

Shake all ingredients with ice
and strain into a shooter glass.
Top with a capful of Bromo-
Seltzer.

Helicopter
½ oz. Green Chartreuse
½ oz. Bacardi 151 Rum

Layer ingredients in order
given in a shot glass. Ignite
with a match.

Hell Razor
¾ oz. Jack Daniel's
¾ oz. Tequila
¾ oz. Vodka

Shake all ingredients with ice
and strain into a shooter glass.

Hemorrhaging Brain
1 oz. Strawberry Schnapps
½ oz. Baileys Irish Cream

Pour schnapps in a shooter
glass. Pour Baileys in the
center of the schnapps.
Top with a dash of Grenadine.

High Octane
1 ½ oz. Jack Daniel's
½ oz. Cola

Shake both ingredients with
ice and strain into a shooter
glass.

Highway One
1 oz. Vodka
1 oz. Wilderberry Schnapps
½ oz. Lemonade
½ oz. Pineapple Juice

Shake all ingredients with ice
and strain into a shooter glass.

Hitler
½ oz. Goldschlager
½ oz. Jägermeister

Combine both ingredients in a
shot glass.

Hoffa
1 oz. Grain Alcohol
1 oz. Gatorade
1 tbs. Karo Syrup

Shake all ingredients with ice
and strain into a shooter glass.

Hole
1 oz. Baileys Irish Cream
½ oz. Light Rum
½ oz. Vodka

Shake all ingredients with ice
and strain into a shooter glass.

Hole-In-One Shooter
1 ½ oz. Melon Liqueur
¾ oz. Apple Brandy
¼ oz. Cream

Shake all ingredients with ice
and strain into a shooter glass.

Holly by the Beach
¾ oz. Malibu Rum
¾ oz. Watermelon Schnapps
¾ oz. Pineapple Juice

Shake all ingredients with ice
and strain into a shooter glass.

Hollywood
¾ oz. Stolichnaya Vodka
¾ oz. Chambord
¾ oz. Cranberry Juice

Shake all ingredients with ice
and strain into a shooter glass.

Hollywood Popper
1 oz. Vodka
½ oz. Cranberry Juice
Dash of Grenadine

Combine all ingredients in a
shooter glass.

Holy Hand Grenade
1 oz. Absolut Kurant Vodka
1 oz. Chambord
1 oz. Lemonade

Shake all ingredients with ice
and strain into a shooter glass.

Holy Moley
1 ½ oz. Rum
½ oz. Dark Creme de Cacao
½ oz. Kahlua
¼ oz. Triple Sec

Shake all ingredients with ice
and strain into a shooter glass.

Honey Drop
¾ oz. Baileys Irish Cream
¾ oz. Butterscotch Schnapps
¾ oz. Vodka
1 oz. Cream

Shake all ingredients with ice
and strain into a shooter glass.

Honey Melon
1 oz. Honey Liqueur
¼ oz. Vodka
½ oz. Melon Liqueur
½ oz. Cranberry Juice
½ oz. Pineapple Juice

Shake all ingredients with ice
and strain into a shooter glass.

Honolulu Hammer
1 ½ oz. Vodka
½ oz. Amaretto
1 oz. Pineapple Juice
¼ oz. Grenadine

Shake all ingredients with ice
and strain into a shooter glass.

Hooter
1 oz. Amaretto
1 oz. Vodka
1 oz. Orange Juice
¼ oz. Grenadine

Shake all ingredients with ice
and strain into a shooter glass.

Horny Monkey
¾ oz. Kahlua
¾ oz. Green Creme de
Menthe
¾ oz. Creme de Banana
¾ oz. Baileys Irish Cream

Shake all ingredients with ice
and strain into a shooter glass.

Horny Toad
½ oz. Midori Melon Liqueur
½ oz. Southern Comfort
½ oz. Malibu Rum
½ oz. Pineapple Juice
½ oz. 7-Up

Shake all ingredients with ice
and strain into a shooter glass.

Hot & Creamy
1 oz. After Shock Cinnamon
Liqueur
½ oz. Vodka
1 ½ oz. Cream

Shake all ingredients with ice
and strain into a shooter glass.

Hot Apple Pie
1 ½ oz. Sour Apple Pucker
Schnapps
½ oz. Hot Damn Cinnamon
Schnapps

Combine both ingredients in a
shooter glass.

Hot Bitch
1 oz. After Shock Cinnamon
Liqueur
1 oz. Hot Damn Cinnamon
Schnapps
3 Dashes Tabasco Sauce

Shake all ingredients with ice
and strain into a shooter glass.

Hot Blood
1 ½ oz. After Shock
Cinnamon Liqueur
2 drops Tabasco Sauce

Combine both ingredients in a
large shot glass.

Hot Bomb
1 oz. Cinnamon Schnapps
1 oz. Tequila

Shake both ingredients with
ice and strain into a shooter
glass.

Hot Cherry
½ oz. Black Velvet
½ oz. Amaretto

Combine both ingredients in a
shot glass.

Hot Cherry Pie
1 oz. Hot Damn Cinnamon
Schnapps
1 oz. Cheri-Beri Pucker
Schnapps

Shake both ingredients with
ice and strain into a shooter
glass.

Hot Jizz
½ oz. Cinnamon Schnapps
½ oz. Baileys Irish Cream

Layer ingredients in order
given in a shot glass.

Hot Jose
1 oz. Hot Damn Cinnamon
Schnapps
1 oz. Cuervo Gold Tequila

Combine both ingredients in a
shooter glass.

Hot Love
1 ½ oz. Amaretto
1 ½ oz. Hot Coffee

Combine both ingredients in a
shooter glass.

Hot Pussy
½ oz. Cinnamon Schnapps
1 oz. Passion Fruit Liqueur
2 Dashes Tabasco Sauce

Shake all ingredients with ice
and strain into a shooter glass.

Hot Shot
1 ½ oz. Grand Marnier
1 ½ oz. Cold Coffee

Shake both ingredients with
ice and strain into a shooter
glass.

Hot Shots
½ oz. Vodka
½ oz. Peppermint Schnapps
Dash of Tabasco Sauce

Combine all ingredients in a
shot glass.

Huckleberry Hound Dog
1 oz. Raspberry Schnapps
1 oz. Light Creme de Cacao
1 oz. Cream

Shake all ingredients with ice
and strain into a shooter glass.

Hurricane
1 ¼ oz. Rum
1 ½ oz. Sour Mix
¾ oz. Apricot Brandy
1 oz. Orange Juice
Dash of Grenadine

Shake all ingredients with ice
and strain into a shooter glass.

Hussie
1 oz. Amaretto
1 oz. Draft Beer
1 oz. Sour Mix

Shake all ingredients with ice
and strain into a shooter glass.

Ice
1 oz. Goldschlager
1 oz. Grain Alcohol

Shake both ingredients with
ice and strain into a shooter
glass.

Icebreaker
1 ¼ oz. Rumple Minze
1 ¼ oz. Yukon Jack

Shake both ingredients with
ice and strain into a shooter
glass.

Iced Cafe
1 ¼ oz. Coffee Liqueur
1 oz. Cream
2 oz. Cold Coffee

Shake all ingredients with ice
and strain into a shooter glass.

Idori
½ oz. Light Creme de Cacao
½ oz. Grand Marnier
½ oz. Strawberry Liqueur
1 oz. Cream

Shake all ingredients with ice
and strain into a shooter glass.

Ike Turner
1 oz. Hennessy VS
1 oz. Tanqueray Gin
1 oz. Courvoisier VS

Stir all ingredients with ice
and strain into a shooter glass.

Illusion
½ oz. Vodka
½ oz. Light Rum
½ oz. Tequila
½ oz. Melon Liqueur
½ oz. Triple Sec

Shake all ingredients with ice
and strain into a shooter glass.

In Between
1 oz. Peppermint Schnapps
1 oz. Vodka

Layer ingredients in order
given in a shooter glass.
Top with 3 drops Tabasco
Sauce.

Inch & a Half
1 oz. Tequila
1 oz. Triple Sec
1 oz. Lime Cordial

Shake all ingredients with ice
and strain into a shooter glass.

Inspiration Point
¾ oz. Melon Liqueur
¾ oz. Vodka
¾ oz. Raspberry Schnapps
¾ oz. Cranberry Juice

Shake all ingredients with ice
and strain into a shooter glass.

Instant Orgasm
½ oz. Vodka
½ oz. Kahlua
½ oz. Baileys Irish Cream
½ oz. Amaretto
½ oz. Frangelico

Shake all ingredients with ice
and strain into a shooter glass.

International Incident
½ oz. Baileys Irish Cream
¼ oz. Vodka
¼ oz. Coffee Liqueur
¼ oz. Amaretto
¼ oz. Hazelnut Liqueur

Shake all ingredients with ice
and strain into a shooter glass.

IRA
1 oz. Irish Whiskey
1 oz. Irish Mist
1 oz. Baileys Irish Cream

Shake all ingredients with ice
and strain into a shooter glass.

IRA Bomber
½ oz. Baileys Irish Cream
½ oz. Vodka

Layer ingredients in order
given in a shot glass.

Iranian Quaalude
½ oz. Frangelico
½ oz. Baileys Irish Cream
½ oz. Amaretto
½ oz. Kahlua
½ oz. Vodka

Shake all ingredients with ice
and strain into a shooter glass.

Irish Berry Blast
1 oz. Midori Melon Liqueur
1 oz. Raspberry Schnapps
1 oz. Cranberry Juice
¾ oz. Baileys Irish Cream
Splash of Orange Juice

Shake all ingredients with ice
and strain into a shooter glass.

Irish Candy
¾ oz. Baileys Irish Cream
¾ oz. Raspberry Schnapps
¾ oz. Kahlua
¾ oz. Light Creme de Cacao

Shake all ingredients with ice
and strain into a shooter glass.

Irish Eyes
1 oz. Green Creme de Menthe
1 oz. Irish Whiskey
1 oz. Cream

Shake all ingredients with ice
and strain into a shooter glass.

Irish Flag
1 oz. Green Creme de Menthe
1 oz. Baileys Irish Cream
1 oz. Grand Marnier

Layer ingredients in order
given in a shooter glass.

Irish Headlock
½ oz. Irish Whiskey
½ oz. Baileys Irish Cream
½ oz. Amaretto di Saronno
½ oz. Brandy

Shake all ingredients with ice
and strain into a shooter glass.

Irish Love Potion
1 ½ oz. Baileys Irish Cream
1 oz. Irish Mist
1 oz. Cranberry Juice

Shake all ingredients with ice
and strain into a shooter glass.

Irish Monk
¾ oz. Frangelico
¾ oz. Peppermint Schnapps
¾ oz. Baileys Irish Cream

Layer ingredients in order
given in a shooter glass.

Irish Monkey
1 oz. Kahlua
1 oz. Baileys Irish Cream
1 oz. Creme de Banana

Shake all ingredients with ice
and strain into a shooter glass.

Irish Nut
1 ½ oz. Baileys Irish Cream
1 ½ oz. Frangelico

Shake both ingredients with
ice and strain into a shooter
glass.

Irish Quaalude
½ oz. Baileys Irish Cream
½ oz. Vodka
½ oz. Frangelico
½ oz. Light Creme de Cacao

Shake all ingredients with ice
and strain into a shooter glass.

Irish Sunrise
¼ oz. Grenadine
¾ oz. Creme de Banana
¾ oz. Amaretto
¾ oz. Baileys Irish Cream

Layer ingredients in order
given in a shooter glass.

Irish Sunset
¾ oz. Amaretto
¾ oz. Creme de Banana
¾ oz. Baileys Irish Cream

Layer ingredients in order
given in a shooter glass.

Irish Widow
1 ¼ oz. White Sambuca
1 oz. Baileys Irish Cream

Layer ingredients in order
given in a shooter glass.

Iron Cross
1 ½ oz. Peppermint Schnapps
1 ½ oz. Apricot Brandy

Shake both ingredients with
ice and strain into a shooter
glass.

Iron Curtain
1 oz. Jägermeister
1 oz. Bacardi 151 Rum

Layer ingredients in order
given in a shooter glass.

Ironman
½ oz. Green Chartreuse
½ oz. White Sambuca
½ oz. Scotch
½ oz. Tequila
½ oz. Tabasco Sauce

Shake all ingredients with ice
and strain into a shooter glass.

Island Mist
½ oz. Light Creme de Cacao
½ oz. Frangelico
½ oz. Baileys Irish Cream

Layer ingredients in order
given in a shooter glass.
Top with a sprinkle of ground
cinnamon.

It Will Make You Shit
2 oz. Vodka
½ oz. Tabasco Sauce
Dash of Honey
1 raw Egg
Pinch of Instant Coffee
Powder

Shake all ingredients well
with ice and strain into a
shooter glass.

Italian Ice
1 oz. Vodka
1 oz. Blue Curacao
¼ oz. 7-Up
¼ oz. Sour Mix

Shake all ingredients with ice
and strain into a shooter glass.

Italian Surfer
1 oz. Amaretto
1 oz. Malibu Rum
1 oz. Pineapple Juice
Dash of Grenadine

Shake all ingredients with ice
and strain into a shooter glass.

Italian Surfer on Acid
¾ oz. Amaretto
¾ oz. Jägermeister
¾ oz. Malibu Rum
¾ oz. Pineapple Juice

Shake all ingredients with ice
and strain into a shooter glass.

Italian Valium
1 oz. Amaretto
1 oz. Crown Royal

Layer ingredients in order
given in a shooter glass.

**Jack & Gin Went Up the
Hill**
1 oz. Jack Daniel's
1 oz. Gin
1 Ice Cube

Combine all ingredients in a
shooter glass.

Jack Meoff
1 ½ oz. Applejack
½ oz. Midori Melon Liqueur
3 oz. 7-Up

Stir all ingredients with ice
and strain into a shooter glass.

Jack Rabbit
¾ oz. Yukon Jack
½ oz. Cherry Brandy
1 ¼ oz. Sour Mix

Shake all ingredients with ice
and strain into a shooter glass.

Jackhammer
1 ½ oz. Yukon Jack
1 ½ oz. Peppermint Schnapps

Shake both ingredients with
ice and strain into a shooter
glass.

Jackson 5
½ oz. Jim Beam
½ oz. Jack Daniel's
½ oz. Tequila
½ oz. Jägermeister
½ oz. Rye Whiskey

Shake all ingredients with ice
and strain into a shooter glass.

Jade Monkey
1 oz. Tequila
¼ oz. Lime Juice
2 oz. Lime Kool-Aid
1 tsp. Vanilla Extract

Shake all ingredients with ice
and strain into a shooter glass.

Jagerita
¾ oz. Jägermeister
¾ oz. Tequila
¾ oz. Lime Juice

Shake all ingredients with ice
and strain into a shooter glass.

Jagerschlager
1 oz. Jägermeister
1 oz. Goldschlager

Layer ingredients in order
given in a shooter glass.

Jamaican Dust
1 oz. Dark Rum
½ oz. Tia Maria
½ oz. Pineapple Juice
½ oz. Orange Juice

Shake all ingredients with ice
and strain into a shooter glass.

Jamaican Monkey Fuck
¾ oz. Malibu Rum
¾ oz. Tia Maria
¾ oz. Creme de Banana

Shake all ingredients with ice
and strain into a shooter glass.

Jamaican Tennis Beads
½ oz. Smirnoff Vodka
½ oz. Malibu Rum
½ oz. Chambord
½ oz. Creme de Banana
½ oz. Pineapple Juice
½ oz. Cream

Shake all ingredients with ice
and strain into a shooter glass.

Jambalaya
¾ oz. Southern Comfort
¾ oz. Peach Schnapps
¾ oz. Sour Mix
Dash of Grenadine

Shake all ingredients with ice
and strain into a shooter glass.

Jameson's Sour Melon
1 oz. Jameson Irish Whiskey
¼ oz. Melon Liqueur
¼ oz. Sour Mix
½ oz. Orange Juice
½ oz. Pineapple Juice

Shake all ingredients with ice
and strain into a shooter glass.

Jawbreaker
1 oz. Cinnamon Schnapps
½ oz. Tabasco Sauce

Combine both ingredients in a
large shot glass.

Jekyll & Hyde Cyber Shot
1 oz. Jägermeister
1 oz. Dr. McGillicuddy's
Menthomint Schnapps

Layer ingredients in order
given in a shooter glass.

Jedi Mind Trick
¾ oz. Goldschlager
¾ oz. Baileys Irish Cream
¾ oz. Melon Liqueur
¾ oz. Rum

Shake all ingredients with ice
and strain into a shooter glass.

Jefferson Blues
¾ oz. Blue Curacao
¾ oz. Wilderberry Schnapps
¾ oz. Absolut Vodka
¾ oz. Sour Mix
Splash of 7-Up

Shake all ingredients with ice
and strain into a shooter glass.

Jelly Doughnut
½ oz. White Sambuca
1 oz. Chambord
½ oz. Baileys Irish Cream

Layer ingredients in order
given in a shooter glass.

Jellybean
1 oz. Anisette
1 oz. Tequila
1 oz. Grenadine

Shake all ingredients with ice
and strain into a shooter glass.

Jellyfish
¾ oz. White Creme de
Menthe
¾ oz. Amaretto
¾ oz. Baileys Irish Cream

Shake all ingredients with ice
and strain into a shooter glass.
Top with a dash of Grenadine.

Jet Fuel
½ oz. Bacardi Light Rum
½ oz. Captain Morgan Parrot
Bay Rum
½ oz. Nassau Royale Liqueur
½ oz. Bacardi 151 Rum
Dash of Grenadine
1 oz. Pineapple Juice
Splash of 7-Up

Shake all ingredients with ice
and strain into a

Jizz
1 oz. Cognac
½ oz. Baileys Irish Cream
3 oz. Cream

Shake all ingredients with ice
and strain into a shooter glass.

John Lennon
1 oz. White Sambuca
1 oz. Bacardi 151 Rum

Layer ingredients in order
given in a shooter glass.

Johnny Appleseed
1 oz. Peach Schnapps
½ oz. Vodka
¼ oz. Chambord
¼ oz. Melon Liqueur
Splash of Pineapple Juice

Shake all ingredients with ice
and strain into a shooter glass.

Johnny Hot
¾ oz. Rumple Minze
¾ oz. Green Chartreuse
½ oz. Bourbon
½ oz. Blackberry Liqueur
½ oz. Beer

Shake all ingredients with ice
and strain into a shooter glass.

Johnny on the Beach
¾ oz. Vodka
½ oz. Melon Liqueur
½ oz. Black Raspberry
Liqueur
¼ oz. Pineapple Juice
¼ oz. Orange Juice
¼ oz. Grapefruit Juice
¼ oz. Cranberry Juice

Shake all ingredients with ice
and strain into a shooter glass.

Jolly Mon
1 oz. Dark Rum
1 oz. Malibu Rum
1 oz. Coco Lopez
½ oz. Cream

Shake all ingredients with ice
and strain into a shooter glass.
Top with shredded coconut.

Jolly Rancher
1 oz. Melon Liqueur
1 oz. Apple Schnapps
1 oz. Sour Mix

Shake all ingredients with ice
and strain into a shooter glass.
Top with a splash of club
soda.

Jolly Roger
1 oz. Captain Morgan Spiced
Rum
1 oz. Cinnamon Schnapps

Shake both ingredients with
ice and strain into a shooter
glass.

Jose's Cum
¾ oz. Cuervo Gold Tequila
¾ oz. Butterscotch Schnapps
¾ oz. Baileys Irish Cream

Layer ingredients in order
given in a shooter glass.

Juicy Fruit
¾ oz. Melon Liqueur
½ oz. Creme de Banana
½ oz. Licor 43
¼ oz. Blackberry Brandy
¼ oz. Pineapple Juice
¼ oz. Cream

Shake all ingredients with ice
and strain into a shooter glass.

Jump Shot
¾ oz. Light Rum
½ oz. Orange Curacao
1 oz. Pineapple Juice
2 Dashes Bitters

Shake all ingredients with ice
and strain into a shooter glass.

Jumping Bean
1 ½ oz. Tequila
1 oz. White Sambuca

Shake both ingredients with
ice and strain into a shooter
glass. Float 3 coffee beans on
top.

Kahlua Candy Cane
1 oz. Kahlua
1 oz. Peppermint Schnapps
1 oz. Cream

Shake all ingredients with ice
and strain into a shooter glass.

Kahlua Slam
½ oz. Kahlua
½ oz. Tequila

Layer ingredients in order
given in a shot glass.

Kali Pie
½ oz. Licor 43
½ oz. Cream
½ oz. Lime Juice
½ oz. Sour Mix

Shake all ingredients with ice
and strain into a shooter glass.

Kamikaze
1 oz. Vodka
1 oz. Triple Sec
1 oz. Lime Juice

Shake all ingredients with ice
and strain into a shooter glass.

KAT
1 oz. Kahlua
1 oz. Anisette
1 oz. Tequila

Shake all ingredients with ice
and strain into a shooter glass.

Kentucky Blue Streak
1 oz. Baileys Irish Cream
1 oz. Light Creme de Cacao
1 oz. Blue Curacao

Shake all ingredients with ice
and strain into a shooter glass.

Kentucky Twister
1 oz. Wild Turkey
1 oz. Jim Beam
1 oz. Mountain Dew

Combine all ingredients in a
shooter glass.

Kermit's Rainbow
½ oz. Grenadine
½ oz. Kahlua
½ oz. Blue Curacao
½ oz. Baileys Irish Cream
½ oz. Grand Marnier
½ oz. Bacardi Light Rum

Layer ingredients in order
given in a shooter glass.

Key Lime Pie
1 oz. Licor 43
1 oz. Amaretto
¼ oz. Triple Sec
Dash of Lime Juice
Dash of Cream

Shake all ingredients with ice
and strain into a shooter glass.

Key West Oyster Shooter
1 oz. Bloody Mary Mix
1 oz. Peach Schnapps
1 shucked Oyster
Dash of Tabasco Sauce
Pinch of Black Pepper

Combine all ingredients in a
shooter glass.

KGB
¾ oz. Kahlua
¾ oz. Green Creme de
Menthe
¾ oz. Baileys Irish Cream

Layer ingredients in order
given in a shooter glass.

Kick in the Balls
1 oz. Jack Daniel's
1 oz. Tequila

Shake both ingredients with
ice and strain into a shooter
glass.

Kicker
1 oz. Kahlua
1 oz. Amaretto
1 oz. Grand Marnier

Shake all ingredients with ice
and strain into a shooter glass.

Killer
1 oz. Bacardi 151 Rum
1 oz. 100 Proof Vodka
1 oz. Tequila

Shake all ingredients with ice
and strain into a shooter glass.

Killer Bee
1 oz. Jägermeister
1 oz. Honey

Shake both ingredients with
ice and strain into a shooter
glass.

Killer Kool-Aid
½ oz. Southern Comfort
½ oz. Melon Liqueur
½ oz. Vodka
½ oz. Amaretto
½ oz. Cranberry Juice

Shake all ingredients with ice
and strain into a shooter glass.

Kinky Bryan
1 oz. Yukon Jack
½ oz. Creme de Banana
¼ oz. Creme de Almond
1 ¼ oz. Orange Juice

Shake all ingredients with ice
and strain into a shooter glass.

Kiss of Death
¾ oz. Tequila
¾ oz. Jack Daniel's
¾ oz. Dark Rum

Combine all ingredients in a
shooter glass.

Kiwi
1 oz. Strawberry Schnapps
½ oz. Banana Schnapps
1 oz. Orange Juice

Shake all ingredients with ice
and strain into a shooter glass.

KKK
2 oz. Light Rum
1 oz. Cream

Shake both ingredients with
ice and strain into a shooter
glass. Float a miniature Ritz
cracker on top.

Klingon Battlejuice
1 ½ oz. Vodka
¾ oz. Lemon Juice
Pinch of Ascorbic Acid
(Vitamin C)

Shake all ingredients with ice
and strain into a shooter glass.

Knocker
1 oz. Peach Liqueur
1 oz. Tequila
1 oz. 7-Up

Combine all ingredients in a
shooter glass.

Ko-Cane
1 oz. Kahlua
1 oz. Amaretto
1 oz. Tequila

Shake all ingredients with ice
and strain into a shooter glass.

Kojak
1 oz. Whiskey
½ oz. Dark Rum
1 oz. 7-Up
½ oz. Pineapple Juice

Shake all ingredients with ice
and strain into a shooter glass.

Kooch
1 oz. Baileys Irish Cream
1 oz. Light Creme de Cacao

Shake both ingredients with
ice and strain into a shooter
glass. Top with a sprinkle of
ground cinnamon.

Kool-Aid
1 oz. Melon Liqueur
1 oz. Raspberry Liqueur
1 oz. Cranberry Juice

Shake all ingredients with ice
and strain into a shooter glass.

Kryptonite
1 oz. Green Creme de Menthe
½ oz. Bacardi 151 Rum
½ oz. Vodka
¼ oz. Cream

Shake all ingredients with ice
and strain into a shooter glass.

Kung Fu Chocolate
1 ½ oz. Smirnoff Vodka
1 oz. Bacardi Light Rum
1 scoop Vanilla Ice Cream
1 tsp. Nestle's Quik Powder

Combine all ingredients in a
shooter glass and stir.

L.A. Duster
½ oz. Green Creme de
Menthe
½ oz. Gold Tequila

Layer ingredients in order
given in a shot glass.

L-17
1 oz. Vodka
1 oz. Kahlua
1 oz. Cream
½ oz. Grand Marnier

Layer ingredients in order
given in a shooter glass.

La Bamba
1 oz. Vodka
1 oz. Frangelico
1 oz. Orange Juice

Shake all ingredients with ice
and strain into a shooter glass.

La Bomba
1 oz. Tia Maria
1 oz. Jack Daniel's

Layer ingredients in order
given in a shooter glass.

La Pussy
1 oz. Bacardi Light Rum
1 oz. Cointreau
1 oz. Brandy
¼ oz. Apple Schnapps

Shake all ingredients with ice
and strain into a shooter glass.

Land Mine
1 oz. Bacardi 151 Rum
1 oz. Jägermeister

Shake both ingredients with
ice and strain into a shooter
glass.

Landslide
1 oz. Southern Comfort
1 oz. Tanqueray Gin
1 oz. Pineapple Juice

Shake all ingredients with ice
and strain into a shooter glass.

Laser Beam
¾ oz. Jack Daniel's
¾ oz. Amaretto
¾ oz. Galliano
¾ oz. Peppermint Schnapps

Shake all ingredients with ice
and strain into a shooter glass.

Laser Disk
½ oz. Cutty Sark
½ oz. Drambuie
½ oz. Lemonade

Shake all ingredients with ice
and strain into a large shot
glass.

Laughing All the Way
1 oz. Melon Liqueur
1 oz. Blue Curacao
1 oz. Lemonade

Shake all ingredients with ice
and strain into a shooter glass.

Lava Lamp
1 ½ oz. Vodka
1 ½ oz. Hot Damn Cinnamon
Schnapps

Combine both ingredients in a
shooter glass. Top with a few
drops of Tabasco Sauce.

**Lay Me Down on the
Bathroom Floor Naked**
¾ oz. Jägermeister
¾ oz. Rumple Minze
¾ oz. Stolichnaya Vodka
¾ oz. Bacardi 151 Rum

Shake all ingredients with ice
and strain into a shooter glass.

**Lead Me Down the Alley
Sweet Jesus**
¾ oz. Jägermeister
¾ oz. White Sambuca
¾ oz. Rumple Minze

Shake all ingredients with ice
and strain into a shooter glass.

Lemon Drop
1 ¼ oz. Absolut Citron Vodka

Stir vodka with ice and strain
into a shooter glass. Serve
with a sugar-coated lemon
wedge.

Lemon Kamikaze
1 oz. Absolut Citron Vodka
1 oz. Triple Sec
1 oz. Lemon Juice

Shake all ingredients with ice
and strain into a shooter glass.

Lemon Pine Sol
1 oz. Gin
1 oz. Lemon Juice
1 oz. Club Soda

Stir all ingredients with ice
and strain into a shooter glass.

Leprechaun's Gold
1 oz. Goldschlager
1 oz. Green Chartreuse
1 oz. Lime Juice

Shake all ingredients with ice
and strain into a shooter glass.

Leprechaun's Libation
1 ½ oz. Baileys Irish Cream
1 ½ oz. Brandy

Shake both ingredients with
ice and strain into a shooter
glass.

Leprechaun's Lunch
½ oz. Green Creme de
Menthe
½ oz. Dark Creme de Cacao
½ oz. Baileys Irish Cream

Layer ingredients in order
given in a shooter glass.

Letter Bomb
1 oz. Irish Whiskey
1 oz. Irish Mist
1 oz. Baileys Irish Cream

Shake all ingredients with ice
and strain into a shooter glass.

Lewinsky Blowjob
½ oz. Amaretto
½ oz. Grain Alcohol
½ oz. Bacardi 151 Rum
1 oz. Cola

Shake all ingredients with ice
and strain into a shooter glass.

Licorice Lix
1 ¼ oz. White Sambuca
¾ oz. Orange Juice

Shake both ingredients with
ice and strain into a shooter
glass.

Licorice Stick
½ oz. Anisette
½ oz. Triple Sec
1 oz. Vodka

Shake all ingredients with ice
and strain into a shooter glass.

Lifesaver
1 oz. Butterscotch Schnapps
1 oz. Baileys Irish Cream

Layer ingredients in order
given in a shooter glass.

Lime Sweet Tart
1 oz. Vodka
1 oz. Lime Juice
1 oz. Grenadine

Shake all ingredients with ice
and strain into a shooter glass.

Limedrop
1 oz. Vodka
1 oz. Triple Sec
1 oz. Limeade

Shake all ingredients with ice
and strain into a shooter glass.

Lion Tamer
1 ¼ oz. Southern Comfort
½ oz. Lime Juice

Shake both ingredients with
ice and strain into a shooter
glass.

Lip Balm
1 ½ oz. Whiskey
½ oz. Dark Rum
½ oz. Coco Lopez
½ oz. Light Creme de Cacao

Shake all ingredients with ice
and strain into a shooter glass.

Liquid Bitch
1 oz. Vodka
1 oz. Peppermint Schnapps
1 oz. Bacardi 151 Rum

Shake all ingredients with ice
and strain into a shooter glass.

Liquid Candy Cane
1 ½ oz. Firewater Cinnamon
Schnapps
1 ½ oz. Rumple Minze

Shake both ingredients with
ice and strain into a shooter
glass.

Liquid Cocaine
1 oz. Jägermeister
1 oz. Rumple Minze
1 oz. Bacardi 151 Rum

Shake all ingredients with ice
and strain into a shooter glass.

Liquid Coma
1 ½ oz. Dark Rum
½ oz. Southern Comfort
½ oz. Dark Creme de Cacao

Shake all ingredients with ice
and strain into a shooter glass.

Liquid Crack
½ oz. Firewater Cinnamon
Schnapps
½ oz. Bacardi 151 Rum
½ oz. Jägermeister
½ oz. Rumple Minze

Shake all ingredients with ice
and strain into a shooter glass.

Liquid Drano
1 oz. Bourbon
1 oz. Scotch
1 oz. Beer
1 oz. Whiskey
1 oz. Wine

Pour each ingredient in
separate shot glasses. Drink in
order.

Liquid Heroin
1 oz. Rumple Minze
1 oz. Jägermeister
1 oz. Bacardi 151 Rum

Layer ingredients in order
given in a shooter glass.

Liquid Pants Remover
½ oz. Amaretto
½ oz. Dark Rum
½ oz. Southern Comfort
½ oz. Tequila
½ oz. Vodka

Shake all ingredients with ice
and strain into a shooter glass.
Top with a splash of cola.

Liquid Turd
¾ oz. Baileys Irish Cream
¾ oz. Bacardi 151 Rum
½ oz. Cola

Combine all ingredients in a
shooter glass.

Liquid Valium
¾ oz. Bacardi 151 Rum
½ oz. Triple Sec
¼ oz. Creme de Banana
½ oz. Pineapple Juice
½ oz. Cream

Shake all ingredients with ice
and strain into a shooter glass.

Listerine
1 ½ oz. Ice 101 Peppermint
Schnapps
½ oz. Blue Curacao

Shake both ingredients with
ice and strain into a shooter
glass.

Little Beer
1 oz. Licor 43
Dash of Cream

Layer ingredients in order
given in a shot glass.

Little Piece of Hell
1 ½ oz. Hot Damn Cinnamon
Schnapps
1 ½ oz. Light Corn Syrup

Combine both ingredients in a
shooter glass.

Little Red S-10
¾ oz. Hot Damn Cinnamon
Schnapps
¾ oz. Sour Apple Pucker
Schnapps
¾ oz. Smirnoff Vodka

Shake all ingredients with ice
and strain into a shooter glass.
Top with a dash of whipped
cream.

Lobotomy
¾ oz. Chambord
¾ oz. Amaretto
¾ oz. Pineapple Juice

Shake all ingredients with ice
and strain into a shooter glass.

Loch Ness Monster
Splash of 7-Up
¾ oz. Midori Melon Liqueur
¾ oz. Baileys Irish Cream
¾ oz. Jägermeister

Layer ingredients in order
given in a shooter glass.

London Pummel
1 oz. Gin
Dash of Lime Juice
1 oz. Tonic Water

Combine all ingredients in a
shooter glass.

Look Out Below
1 ½ oz. Bacardi 151 Rum
Dash of Lime Juice
Dash of Grenadine

Shake all ingredients with ice
and strain into a shooter glass.

Loopie
1 oz. Vodka
1 oz. Amaretto
1 oz. Pineapple Juice
Dash of Grenadine

Shake all ingredients with ice
and strain into a shooter glass.

Lounge Singer
1 oz. Goldschlager
1 oz. Apple Schnapps
½ oz. Cream

Shake all ingredients with ice
and strain into a shooter glass.

Love in a Hot Tub
½ oz. Peppermint Schnapps
½ oz. Crown Royal
½ oz. Bacardi 151 Rum
½ oz. Baileys Irish Cream

Layer ingredients in order
given in a shooter glass.

Lube Job
1 ½ oz. Vodka
1 oz. Baileys Irish Cream

Stir both ingredients with ice
and strain into a shooter glass.

Lucky Charm
1 oz. Kahlua
1 oz. Butterscotch Schnapps
1 oz. Cream
3 drops Green Food Coloring

Shake all ingredients with ice
and strain into a shooter glass.

Lulu
½ oz. Vodka
½ oz. Triple Sec
½ oz. Light Rum
½ oz. Amaretto\
½ oz. Peach Schnapps
1 oz. Sour Mix
Splash of Pineapple Juice

Shake all ingredients with ice
and strain into a shooter glass.
Top with ¼ oz. Grenadine.

Lunch Box
1 oz. Amaretto
2 oz. Beer
2 oz. Orange Juice

Pour amaretto into a shot
glass. Put the shot into a
larger glass. Pour beer around
the shot glass until it almost to
the top of the shot glass. Add
orange juice.

Luscious Lemonade
1 ½ oz. Peach Schnapps
½ oz. Lime Juice

Shake both ingredients with
ice and strain into a shooter
glass.

Lynchburg Lemondrop
1 oz. Jack Daniel's
1 oz. Triple Sec
1 oz. Sour Mix

Shake all ingredients with ice
and strain into a shooter glass.

Madhatter
1 oz. Vodka
1 oz. Peach Schnapps
½ oz. Lemonade
½ oz. Cola

Shake all ingredients with ice
and strain into a shooter glass.

Malibu Barbie
¾ oz. Malibu Rum
¾ oz. Kahlua
¾ oz. Baileys Irish Cream

Shake all ingredients with ice
and strain into a shooter glass.

Malibu Colada
1 oz. Malibu Rum
1 oz. Pineapple Juice
1 oz. Cream

Shake all ingredients with ice
and strain into a shooter glass.

Man with No Name
1 oz. Amaretto
1 oz. Rye Whiskey
1 oz. Sour Mix

Shake all ingredients with ice
and strain into a shooter glass.

Mandeville
1 ½ oz. Light Rum
1 oz. Dark Rum
Dash of Galliano
Dash of Lime Juice
Dash of Cola
Dash of Grenadine

Shake all ingredients with ice
and strain into a shooter glass.

Mango
1 oz. Southern Comfort
¾ oz. Peach Schnapps
¼ oz. Vodka
1 oz. Orange Juice
Dash of Grenadine

Shake all ingredients with ice
and strain into a shooter glass.

Mardi Gras Float
2 oz. Praline Liqueur
1 oz. Vodka

Shake both ingredients with
ice and strain into a shooter
glass. Top with whipped
cream. Garnish with chocolate
shavings and grated coconut.

Martian
½ oz. Cinnamon Schnapps
½ oz. Vodka
½ oz. Lemon Juice
½ oz. 7-Up
½ oz. Lemon-Lime Kool-Aid

Shake all ingredients with ice
and strain into a shooter glass.

Martian Hard On
¾ oz. Green Creme de
Menthe
¾ oz. Baileys Irish Cream
¾ oz. Melon Liqueur

Layer ingredients in order
given in a shooter glass.

Martian Orgasm
1 oz. Melon Liqueur
½ oz. Vodka
½ oz. Peach Schnapps
1 oz. Orange Juice

Shake all ingredients with ice
and strain into a shooter glass.

Matress
¾ oz. Chambord
¾ oz. Vodka
¾ oz. Southern Comfort
¾ oz. Pineapple Juice

Shake all ingredients with ice
and strain into a shooter glass.

Maui Wowie
1 oz. Malibu Rum
½ oz. Melon Liqueur
½ oz. Orange Juice
½ oz. Pineapple Juice

Shake all ingredients with ice
and strain into a shooter glass.
Top with a splash of club
soda.

Mayor's Jellybean
¼ oz. White Sambuca
¾ oz. 100 Proof Southern
Comfort
1 drop Grenadine

Layer ingredients in order
given in a shot glass.

Melaretto
1 ¼ oz. Amaretto
1 ¼ oz. Melon Liqueur

Shake both ingredients with
ice and strain into a shooter
glass.

Melon Ball
1 ½ oz. Melon Liqueur
½ oz. Vodka
1 oz. Pineapple Juice

Shake all ingredients with ice
and strain into a shooter glass.

Melon Chill
1 oz. Melon Liqueur
1 oz. Vodka
½ oz. Lemonade
½ oz. Pineapple Juice

Shake all ingredients with ice
and strain into a shooter glass.

Melon Cooler
1 oz. Melon Liqueur
1 oz. Orange Juice
1 oz. 7-Up

Shake all ingredients with ice
and strain into a shooter glass.

Melon Kamikaze
1 oz. Vodka
1 oz. Melon Liqueur
1 oz. Sour Mix

Shake all ingredients with ice
and strain into a shooter glass.

Melon Lemondrop
1 oz. Melon Liqueur
2 oz. Lemonade

Shake both ingredients with
ice and strain into a shooter
glass.

Melon Limedrop
1 oz. Melon Liqueur
2 oz. Limeade

Shake both ingredients with
ice and strain into a shooter
glass.

Melon Sourball
1 oz. Melon Liqueur
1 oz. Lemonade
1 oz. Orange Juice

Shake all ingredients with ice
and strain into a shooter glass.

Meltdown
1 oz. Vodka
½ oz. Peach Schnapps

Shake both ingredients with
ice and strain into a shooter
glass.

Menagerie
1 oz. Jack Daniel's
1 oz. Southern Comfort
1 oz. Surge Soda

Stir all ingredients with ice
and strain into a shooter glass.

Messy Brains
¾ oz. Grenadine
1 oz. Baileys Irish Cream
¼ oz. Grenadine

Layer ingredients in order
given in a shooter glass.

Mexican
½ oz. Sloe Gin
½ oz. Vodka
½ oz. Melon Liqueur

Layer ingredients in order
given in a shooter glass.

Mexican Bud
1 oz. Budweiser Beer

Pour into a salt-rimmed shot
glass.

Mexican Chiller
1 ¼ oz. Tequila
½ oz. Clamato Juice
Dash of Tabasco Sauce

Shake all ingredients with ice
and strain into a shooter glass.

Mexican Flag
1 oz. Green Creme de Menthe
1 oz. Glayva
1 oz. Tequila

Layer ingredients in order
given in a shooter glass.

Mexican Mayhem
¼ oz. Tabasco Sauce
1 oz. Tequila
¼ oz. Lemon Juice

Layer ingredients in order
given in a shooter glass.

Mexican Missile
¾ oz. Vodka
¾ oz. Tequila
¾ oz. Lime Juice

Shake all ingredients with ice
and strain into a shooter glass.
Top with a splash of club
soda.

Mexican Mother Fucker
½ oz. Baileys Irish Cream
½ oz. Frangelico
½ oz. Kahlua
½ oz. Cuervo 1800 Tequila

Shake all ingredients with ice
and strain into a shooter glass.

Mexican on Crack
¾ oz. Jägermeister
¾ oz. Goldschlager
¾ oz. Tequila

Shake all ingredients with ice
and strain into a shooter glass.

Mexican Snowshoe
1 oz. Green Creme de Menthe
1 oz. Tequila

Shake both ingredients with
ice and strain into a shooter
glass.

Mexicana
1 ½ oz. White Tequila
1 oz. Pineapple Juice
1 oz. Sour Mix
Dash of Grenadine

Shake all ingredients with ice
and strain into a shooter glass.

Miami Ice
½ oz. Vodka
½ oz. Gin
½ oz. Rum
½ oz. Peach Schnapps
½ oz. Cold Tea
½ oz. Sour Mix
½ oz. 7-Up

Shake all ingredients with ice
and strain into a shooter glass.

Miami Vice
1 oz. Vodka
1 oz. Peach Schnapps
1 oz. Orange Juice

Shake all ingredients with ice
and strain into a shooter glass.

Mick Jagger
1 oz. Creme de Banana
½ oz. Vodka
1 ½ oz. Orange Juice

Shake all ingredients with ice
and strain into a shooter glass.

Midnight Cowboy
1 ½ oz. Bourbon
1 oz. Dark Rum
½ oz. Cream

Shake all ingredients with ice
and strain into a shooter glass.

Miles of Smiles
1 oz. Crown Royal
1 oz. Amaretto
1 oz. Rumple Minze

Shake all ingredients with ice
and strain into a shooter glass.

Milky Way
½ oz. Vodka
½ oz. Kahlua
½ oz. Dark Creme de Cacao
1 ½ oz. Cream

Shake all ingredients with ice
and strain into a shooter glass.

Mind Eraser
1 oz. Vodka
1 oz. Kahlua
1 oz. Club Soda

Layer ingredients in order
given in a shooter glass.

Mint Desire
1 oz. Rumple Minze
1 oz. Light Creme de Cacao
1 oz. Cream

Shake all ingredients with ice
and strain into a shooter glass.

Mint Ice Cream
1 oz. Peppermint Schnapps
1 oz. Baileys Irish Cream

Chill schnapps with ice and
strain into a shooter glass.
Float Baileys on top.

Misconavitch
¾ oz. Grand Marnier
¼ oz. Cointreau

Combine both ingredients in a
sugar-rimmed shot glass.
Serve with a lemon wedge.

Mo Bookley
1 oz. Kahlua
1 oz. Peppermint Schnapps
1 oz. Baileys Irish Cream

Shake all ingredients with ice
and strain into a shooter glass.

Mocha Mint
1 oz. Coffee Liqueur
1 oz. Light Creme de Cacao
1 oz. White Creme de Menthe

Shake all ingredients with ice
and strain into a shooter glass.

Model T
1 oz. Kahlua
1 oz. Creme de Banana
1 oz. Baileys Irish Cream

Layer ingredients in order
given in a shooter glass.

Mongoose
1 oz. Creme de Banana
1 oz. Light Creme de Cacao
1 oz. Vodka

Shake all ingredients with ice
and strain into a shooter glass.

Mongrel Dog
1 oz. Bundaberg Dark Rum
1 oz. Tequila
1 oz. Tabasco Sauce

Combine all ingredients in a
shooter glass.

Monica's Blue Dress
1 oz. Razzmatazz
½ oz. Vodka
1 oz. Blue Curacao

Layer ingredients in order
given in a shooter glass.
Float 2 drops of cream on top.

Monkey
1 oz. Grand Marnier
½ oz. Triple Sec
¼ oz. Lime Juice

Shake all ingredients with ice
and strain into a shooter glass.

Monkey Around
¾ oz. Creme de Banana
¾ oz. Kahlua
¾ oz. Rum
¾ oz. Baileys Irish Cream

Shake all ingredients with ice
and strain into a shooter glass.

Monkey Balls
¾ oz. Kahlua
¾ oz. Baileys Irish Cream
¾ oz. Creme de Banana
¾ oz. Cream

Shake all ingredients with ice
and strain into a shooter glass.

Monkey Nut
1 oz. Kahlua
1 oz. Baileys Irish Cream
1 oz. Malibu Rum

Layer ingredients in order
given in a shooter glass.

Monkey Shines
1 oz. Bourbon
1 oz. Creme de Banana
1 oz. Baileys Irish Cream

Shake all ingredients with ice
and strain into a shooter glass.

Monster
½ oz. Vodka
½ oz. Melon Liqueur
½ oz. Blue Curacao
½ oz. Amaretto
½ oz. Crown Royal
½ oz. Orange Juice

Shake all ingredients with ice
and strain into a shooter glass.

Montana Fire
1 oz. Cinnamon Schnapps
1 oz. Peppermint Schnapps
½ oz. Tequila
¼ oz. Tabasco Sauce

Shake all ingredients with ice
and strain into a shooter glass.

Montana Slammer
¾ oz. Jack Daniel's
¾ oz. Peppermint Schnapps
Splash of Club Soda

Combine all ingredients in a
shooter glass.

Montana Stump Puller
2 oz. Canadian Whisky
1 oz. White Creme de Menthe

Stir both ingredients with ice
and strain into a shooter glass.

Moody Blue
1 oz. Amaretto
1 oz. Blueberry Schnapps
1 oz. Gin

Shake all ingredients with ice
and strain into a shooter glass.

Moon Doggie
1 oz. Creme de Banana
½ oz. Light Creme de Cacao
1 ½ oz. Cream

Shake all ingredients with ice
and strain into a shooter glass.

Moon Over Moscow
1 ½ oz. Stolichnaya Vodka
1 oz. Peppermint Schnapps
¼ oz. Strawberry Liqueur

Shake all ingredients with ice
and strain into a shooter glass.

Moose Milk
¾ oz. Vodka
¾ oz. Dark Creme de Cacao
½ oz. Galliano
1 oz. Cream
1 oz. Cola

Shake all ingredients with ice
and strain into a shooter glass.

Morgan Jolly Roger
1 oz. Captain Morgan Spiced
Rum
1 oz. Cinnamon Schnapps

Shake both ingredients with
ice and strain into a shooter
glass.

Morgan Wrench
¾ oz. Captain Morgan Spiced
Rum
¾ oz. Amaretto
½ oz. Dark Creme de Cacao

Layer ingredients in order
given in a shooter glass.

Mound's Bar
1 ¼ oz. Malibu Rum
¾ oz. Dark Creme de Cacao
1 oz. Cream

Shake all ingredients with ice
and strain into a shooter glass.

Mountain Dew
1 oz. Kiwi-Lime Liqueur
1 oz. 7-Up

Combine both ingredients in a
shooter glass.

Mouthwash
1 oz. Absolut Vodka
1 oz. Peppermint Schnapps
½ oz. Green Creme de
Menthe

Shake all ingredients with ice
and strain into a shooter glass.

Mr. Ed
½ oz. Yukon Jack
½ oz. Melon Liqueur
½ oz. Orange Curacao
½ oz. Orange Juice
½ oz. Pineapple Juice
½ oz. Sour Mix

Shake all ingredients with ice
and strain into a shooter glass.

Mud Slide
¾ oz. Baileys Irish Cream
¾ oz. Kahlua
¾ oz. Vodka
¾ oz. Cream

Shake all ingredients with ice
and strain into a shooter glass.

Mud, Blood, & Grass
¾ oz. Kahlua
¾ oz. Cherry Advocaat
¾ oz. Green Creme de
Menthe

Layer ingredients in order
given in a shooter glass.

Muff Dive
½ oz. Baileys Irish Cream
½ oz. Kahlua
Whipped Cream

Squirt some whipped cream
into a martini glass. Place a
shot glass into the whipped
cream, and add Baileys and
Kahlua. Fill the martini glass
with more whipped cream
until it is even with the rim.

Multiple Orgasm
1 oz. Baileys Irish Cream
1 oz. Triple Sec
1 oz. Cream

Shake all ingredients with ice
and strain into a shooter glass.

Multiple Screaming Orgasms
1 oz. Baileys Irish Cream
1 oz. Tia Maria
1 oz. Cointreau

Shake all ingredients with ice and strain into a shooter glass.

Murky Waters
¾ oz. Captain Morgan Spiced Rum
¾ oz. Malibu Rum
¾ oz. Southern Comfort
½ oz. Orange Juice
½ oz. Pineapple Juice

Shake all ingredients with ice and strain into a shooter glass.

Mushroom
¾ oz. Grenadine
¾ oz. Melon Liqueur

Layer ingredients in order given in a shooter glass. Pour ¾ oz. Baileys Irish Cream into the center of the drink.

MX Missile
1 oz. Kahlua
1 oz. Baileys Irish Cream
1 oz. Malibu Rum

Shake all ingredients with ice and strain into a shooter glass.

Natural Disaster
1 ¼ oz. After Shock Cinnamon Liqueur
1 ¼ oz. Avalanche Blue Peppermint Schnapps

Layer ingredients in order given in a shooter glass.

Nazi
¾ oz. Jägermeister
¾ oz. Rumple Minze
¾ oz. Goldschlager

Shake all ingredients with ice and strain into a shooter glass.

Nazi Surfer
1 oz. Jägermeister
¾ oz. Malibu Rum
1 oz. Pineapple Juice

Shake all ingredients with ice and strain into a shooter glass.

Negrita
¾ oz. Pisco Brandy
¾ oz. Coffee Liqueur
¾ oz. Cold Espresso

Shake all ingredients with ice and strain into a shooter glass.

Neon Bull Frog
¾ oz. Melon Liqueur
¾ oz. Blue Curacao
¾ oz. Sour Mix

Shake all ingredients with ice and strain into a shooter glass. Top with a splash of 7-Up.

Neutron Bomb
¾ oz. Kahlua
¾ oz. Baileys Irish Cream
¾ oz. Butterscotch Schnapps

Layer ingredients in order given in a shooter glass.

Newfie
1 oz. Dark Rum
1 oz. Green Creme de Menthe

Layer ingredients in order given in a shooter glass.

Newton Blaster
1 oz. Kahlua
½ oz. Vodka
½ oz. Grand Marnier
½ oz. Baileys Irish Cream

Shake all ingredients with ice and strain into a shooter glass.

Nineteen Eighty-Four
1 oz. Gin
1 oz. Dry Vermouth
½ oz. Southern Comfort
Dash of Pernod

Shake all ingredients with ice and strain into a shooter glass.

Ninja
1 ¼ oz. Jägermeister
1 ¼ oz. Peppermint Schnapps

Shake both ingredients with ice and strain into a shooter glass.

Ninja Turtle
1 ½ oz. Maui Blue Schnapps
1 oz. Orange Juice
1 oz. Pineapple Juice

Shake all ingredients with ice and strain into a shooter glass.

Nipple Dripping
1 ½ oz. Vodka
1 ½ oz. Milk

Stir both ingredients with ice
and strain into a shooter glass.

Nuclear Blue
¾ oz. Blue Curacao
¾ oz. Vodka
¾ oz. Malibu Rum

Shake all ingredients with ice
and strain into a shooter glass.

Nuclear Penguin
1 oz. Vodka
1 oz. Kahlua

Shake both ingredients with
ice and strain into a shooter
glass. Top with a squirt of
whipped cream. Drizzle a
dash of Green Creme de
Menthe on top.

Nuclear Waste
1 ½ oz. Vodka
1 oz. Melon Liqueur
1 oz. Triple Sec
Dash of Lime Juice

Shake all ingredients with ice
and strain into a shooter glass.

Nude Beach
¾ oz. Dark Creme de Cacao
¾ oz. Kahlua
¾ oz. Bacardi Light Rum
Dash of Coco Lopez

Shake all ingredients with ice
and strain into a shooter glass.

Null & Void
1 oz. Vodka
¾ oz. Wilderberry Schnapps
¾ oz. Peach Schnapps
½ oz. Southern Comfort
1 oz. Hawaiian Punch Fruit
Drink

Shake all ingredients with ice
and strain into a shooter glass.

Nutcracker
1 oz. Chambord
1 oz. Frangelico
1 oz. Cream

Shake all ingredients with ice
and strain into a shooter glass.

Nuts & Berries
1 oz. Frangelico
1 oz. Black Raspberry
Liqueur
1 oz. Cream

Shake all ingredients with ice
and strain into a shooter glass.

Nutty Professor
1 oz. Grand Marnier
1 oz. Frangelico
1 oz. Baileys Irish Cream

Shake all ingredients with ice
and strain into a shooter glass.

Nymphomaniac
1 oz. Captain Morgan Spiced
Rum
½ oz. Peach Schnapps
½ oz. Malibu Rum

Shake all ingredients with ice
and strain into a shooter glass.

Nyquil
1 ½ oz. Triple Sec
¾ oz. White Sambuca
¾ oz. Grenadine

Shake all ingredients with ice
and strain into a shooter glass.

Oatmeal Cookie
1 oz. Baileys Irish Cream
1 oz. Goldschlager
1 oz. Butterscotch Schnapps

Shake all ingredients with ice
and strain into a shooter glass.

Oatmeal Raisin Cookie
1 oz. Goldschlager
1 oz. Baileys Irish Cream
1 oz. Jägermeister

Shake all ingredients with ice
and strain into a shooter glass.

O'Blivion
1 oz. Baileys Irish Cream
1 oz. Irish Mist
1 oz. Irish Whiskey

Shake all ingredients with ice
and strain into a shooter glass.

Octopus in the Water
1 oz. Vodka
1 oz. Blue Curacao
½ oz. Sour Mix
½ oz. Lime Juice

Shake all ingredients with ice
and strain into a shooter glass.
Float ½ oz. Wilderberry
Schnapps on top.

Oh My Gosh
1 ½ oz. Amaretto
1 ½ oz. Peach Schnapps

Stir both ingredients with ice
and strain into a shooter glass.

Oil Slick
1 ½ oz. Goldschlager
½ oz. Jack Daniel's

Layer ingredients in order
given in a shooter glass.

Old Hag's Cackle
1 oz. Vodka
1 oz. Raspberry Schnapps
½ oz. Lemonade
½ oz. Orange Juice

Shake all ingredients with ice
and strain into a shooter glass.

O'Leary
1 ½ oz. Absolut Mandarin
Vodka
1 oz. Cranberry Juice
1 oz. Ginger Ale

Stir all ingredients with ice
and strain into a shooter glass.
Drop in a canned mandarin
orange section.

Ooh Baby
1 oz. Apricot Brandy
1 oz. Light Creme de Cacao
½ oz. Triple Sec
½ oz. Orange Juice

Shake all ingredients with ice
and strain into a shooter glass.

Orange Blossom
1 oz. Amaretto
1 oz. Baileys Irish Cream
1 oz. Triple Sec

Shake all ingredients with ice
and strain into a shooter glass.

Orange Blossom Special
1 oz. Smirnoff Vodka
1 oz. Triple Sec
1 oz. Orange Juice

Shake all ingredients with ice
and strain into a shooter glass.

Orange Crush
1 oz. Vodka
1 oz. Triple Sec

Stir both ingredients with ice
and strain into a shooter glass.
Top with a splash of club
soda.

Orange Gallant
¾ oz. Grand Marnier
¾ oz. Galliano
¾ oz. Grenadine
1 oz. Cream

Shake all ingredients with ice
and strain into a shooter glass.

Orange Kamikaze
1 ½ oz. Vodka
½ oz. Triple Sec
1 oz. Orange Juice

Shake all ingredients with ice
and strain into a shooter glass.

Orange Sherbet
¾ oz. Strawberry Liqueur
¾ oz. Peach Schnapps
½ oz. Orange Juice
¾ oz. Cream

Shake all ingredients with ice
and strain into a shooter glass.

Orchid
1 oz. Vodka
1 oz. Peach Schnapps
½ oz. Cherry Juice
½ oz. Orange Juice
½ oz. Cranberry Juice

Shake all ingredients with ice
and strain into a shooter glass.

Oreo Cookie
½ oz. Kahlua
1 oz. Cream
½ oz. Dark Creme de Cacao

Layer ingredients in order
given in a shooter glass.

Orgasm
1 oz. Amaretto
½ oz. Vodka
½ oz. Kahlua
1 oz. Cream

Shake all ingredients with ice
and strain into a shooter glass.

Original Cinn
1 oz. Vodka
1 ½ oz. Cinnamon Schnapps
1 oz. Yukon Jack

Shake all ingredients with ice
and strain into a shooter glass.

Oska-Fagus
¾ oz. Amaretto
¾ oz. Goldschlager
¾ oz. Bacardi 151 Rum

Layer ingredients in order
given in a shooter glass.

Outrigger
1 oz. Light Rum
½ oz. Amaretto di Saronno
1 ½ oz. Cranberry Juice
1 ½ oz. Pineapple Juice

Shake all ingredients with ice
and strain into a shooter glass.
Float ½ oz. Myer's Dark Rum
on top.

Oyster Shooter
1 Shucked Oyster
2 oz. Draft Beer
½ tsp. Horseradish Sauce
2 Dashes Tabasco Sauce

Combine all ingredients in a
shooter glass.

Pacific Pacifier
1 oz. Cointreau
1 oz. Creme de Banana
1 oz. Cream

Shake all ingredients with ice
and strain into a shooter glass.

Paint Ball
½ oz. Creme de Banana
½ oz. Baileys Irish Cream
½ oz. Blue Curacao
½ oz. Southern Comfort
½ oz. Triple Sec

Shake all ingredients with ice
and strain into a shooter glass.

Paintbox
¾ oz. Creme de Banana
¾ oz. Blue Curacao
¾ oz. Cherry Liqueur

Layer ingredients in order
given in a shooter glass.

Pancake
1 oz. Cinnamon Schnapps
1 oz. Baileys Irish Cream
1 oz. Cream

Layer ingredients in order
given in a shooter glass.

Pancho Villa
½ oz. Creme de Almond
½ oz. Tequila
½ oz. Bacardi 151 Rum

Layer ingredients in order
given in a large shot glass.

Paper Bag
1 ½ oz. Whiskey
1 ½ oz. Red Wine

Shake both ingredients with
ice and strain into a shooter
glass.

Paradise Island
1 oz. Apricot Brandy
1 oz. Gin
1 oz. Orange Juice

Shake all ingredients with ice
and strain into a shooter glass.
Top with shredded coconut.

Paradise Punch
½ oz. Stoli Persik Vodka
½ oz. Stoli Razberi Vodka
¼ oz. Triple Sec
Splash of Orange Juice
Splash of Cranberry Juice
Splash of Pineapple Juice

Shake all ingredients with ice
and strain into a shooter glass.

Paralyzer
1 ½ oz. Tequila
½ oz. Light Creme de Cacao
½ oz. Kahlua

Shake all ingredients with ice
and strain into a shooter glass.
Float ½ oz. cream on top.

Paranoia
1 oz. Amaretto
1 oz. Vodka
½ oz. Anisette
½ oz. Orange Juice

Shake all ingredients with ice
and strain into a shooter glass.

Passing Shot
1 ½ oz. Cointreau
½ oz. Campari
1 oz. Apricot Nectar
Dash of Grenadine

Shake all ingredients with ice
and strain into a shooter glass.

Passionate Kiss
1 ½ oz. Vodka
¾ oz. Alize Passion Fruit
Liqueur

Shake both ingredients with
ice and strain into a shooter
glass.

PCB
1 oz. Peppermint Schnapps
1 oz. Cointreau
1 oz. Baileys Irish Cream

Layer ingredients in order
given in a shooter glass.

Peach Bunny
1 oz. Peach Brandy
1 oz. Light Creme de Cacao
1 oz. Cream

Shake all ingredients with ice
and strain into a shooter glass.

Peach Chill
1 oz. Peach Schnapps
1 oz. Vodka
½ oz. Lemonade
½ oz. Pineapple Juice

Shake all ingredients with ice
and strain into a shooter glass.

Peach Cobbler
1 ½ oz. Peach Schnapps
1 ½ oz. Apple Schnapps

Stir both ingredients with ice
and strain into a shooter glass.

Peach Cooler
1 oz. Peach Schnapps
1 oz. Vodka
½ oz. Orange Juice
½ oz. 7-Up

Shake all ingredients with ice
and strain into a shooter glass.

Peach Fuzz
1 ½ oz. Peach Schnapps
1 ½ oz. Cranberry Juice

Shake both ingredients with
ice and strain into a shooter
glass.

Peach Heartburn
1 ½ oz. Peach Schnapps
1 ½ oz. Cola

Shake both ingredients with
ice and strain into a shooter
glass.

Peach Kamikaze
1 oz. Peach Schnapps
1 oz. Triple Sec
1 oz. Sour Mix
Dash of Lime Juice

Shake all ingredients with ice
and strain into a shooter glass.

Peach Lemondrop
1 oz. Peach Schnapps
1 oz. Vodka
1 oz. Lemonade

Shake all ingredients with ice
and strain into a shooter glass.

Peach Limedrop
1 oz. Peach Schnapps
1 oz. Vodka
1 oz. Limeade

Shake all ingredients with ice
and strain into a shooter glass.

Peach on the Beach
1 ½ oz. Vodka
½ oz. Peach Schnapps
¼ oz. Cranberry Juice
¼ oz. Grapefruit Juice

Shake all ingredients with ice
and strain into a shooter glass.

Peach Pirate
1 ½ oz. Peach Schnapps
1 oz. Captain Morgan Spiced
Rum
1 oz. Orange Juice

Shake all ingredients with ice
and strain into a shooter glass.

Peach Sourball
1 oz. Peach Schnapps
1 oz. Vodka
½ oz. Lemonade
½ oz. Orange Juice

Shake all ingredients with ice
and strain into a shooter glass.

Peach Tart
1 ½ oz. Peach Schnapps
¾ oz. Lime Juice

Shake both ingredients with
ice and strain into a shooter
glass.

Peanut Butter & Jelly
¾ oz. Frangelico
¾ oz. Chambord
¾ oz. Baileys Irish Cream

Shake all ingredients with ice
and strain into a shooter glass.

**Peanut Butter Chocolate
Chip Cookie**
1 ½ oz. Frangelico
1 ½ oz. Tia Maria 1 oz.
Kahlua

Shake all ingredients with ice
and strain into a shooter glass.

Pearl Harbor
¾ oz. Midori Melon Liqueur
¾ oz. Vodka
¾ oz. Orange Juice
¾ oz. Pineapple Juice

Shake all ingredients with ice
and strain into a shooter glass.

Pecker Wrecker
½ oz. Blackberry Brandy
½ oz. Creme de Noyeaux
½ oz. Bacardi 151 Rum
¼ oz. Pineapple Juice
¼ oz. Cranberry Juice

Shake all ingredients with ice
and strain into a shooter glass.

Peckerhead
1 oz. Amaretto
1 oz. Yukon Jack
1 oz. Pineapple Juice

Shake all ingredients with ice
and strain into a shooter glass.

Pee Gee
¾ oz. Cinnamon Schnapps
¾ oz. Vodka
¾ oz. Orange Juice

Shake all ingredients with ice
and strain into a shooter glass.

Penalty Shot
1 oz. Kahlua
1 oz. Brandy
½ oz. Grand Marnier

Layer ingredients in order
given in a shooter glass.

Penetrator
1 ½ oz. Vodka
Squeeze of Fresh Lemon Juice

Shake both ingredients with
ice and strain into a sugar-
rimmed shooter glass.
Serve with a lemon wedge.

Penguin
¾ oz. Benedictine
¾ oz. Cherry Liqueur
¾ oz. Gin

Shake all ingredients with ice
and strain into a shooter glass.

Penthouse
1 oz. Vodka
1 oz. Peach Schnapps
1 oz. Cranberry Juice

Shake all ingredients with ice
and strain into a shooter glass.

Peppermint Patty
1 oz. Vodka
½ oz. Peppermint Schnapps
½ oz. Coffee Liqueur

Shake all ingredients with ice
and strain into a shooter glass.

Peppermint Puff
1 ½ oz. Peppermint Schnapps

Chill schnapps with ice and
strain into a shooter glass.
Top with a splash of club
soda.

Peppermint Push
1 oz. Peppermint Schnapps
1 oz. Vodka

Shake both ingredients with
ice and strain into a shooter
glass.

Pepto Pete
1 oz. Grain Alcohol
1 oz. Pepto Bismol

Shake both ingredients with
ice and strain into a shooter
glass.

Photon Torpedoes
1 ¼ oz. Cinnamon Schnapps
1 ¼ oz. Vodka

Shake both ingredients with
ice and strain into a shooter
glass.

Piece of Ass
1 oz. Amaretto
1 oz. Southern Comfort
Splash of Sour Mix

Shake all ingredients with ice
and strain into a shooter glass.

Pierced Buttery Nipple
¾ oz. Butterscotch Schnapps
¾ oz. Baileys Irish Cream
¾ oz. Jägermeister

Layer ingredients in order
given in a shooter glass.

Pigskin Shot
1 oz. Vodka
1 oz. Melon Liqueur
½ oz. Sour Mix

Shake all ingredients with ice
and strain into a shooter glass.

Pimpin'
1 oz. Tequila
1 oz. Whiskey
½ oz. Peach Schnapps

Shake all ingredients with ice
and strain into a shooter glass.

Pine Tree
1 oz. Green Chartreuse
1 oz. Peppermint Schnapps
1 oz. Pineapple Juice

Shake all ingredients with ice
and strain into a shooter glass.

Pineapple Bomb
½ oz. Pineapple Vodka
½ oz. Peach Schnapps
½ oz. Pineapple Juice

Layer ingredients in order
given in a shooter glass.

Pineapple Bomber
¾ oz. Jack Daniel's
¾ oz. Southern Comfort
¾ oz. Pineapple Juice

Shake all ingredients with ice
and strain into a shooter glass.

**Pineapple Upside Down
Cake**
¾ oz. Baileys Irish Cream
¾ oz. Vodka
¾ oz. Butterscotch Schnapps
¾ oz. Pineapple Juice

Shake all ingredients with ice
and strain into a shooter glass.

Pink Panties
1 ½ oz. Tequila
1 ½ oz. Hot Damn Cinnamon
Schnapps

Shake both ingredients with
ice and strain into a shooter
glass.

Pirate's Gold
1 ½ oz. Rum
¾ oz. Goldschlager

Stir both ingredients with ice
and strain into a shooter glass.

Piss Hole in the Snow
1 ½ oz. Light Creme de Cacao
1 oz. White Creme de Menthe
1 ½ oz. Cream

Shake all ingredients with ice
and strain into a shooter glass.
Top with a dash of Galliano.

Pit Bull on Crack
¾ oz. Jägermeister
¾ oz. Rumple Minze
¾ oz. Tequila

Shake all ingredients with ice
and strain into a shooter glass.

Pit of Fire
¼ oz. Tabasco Sauce
1 oz. Bacardi 151 Rum
½ oz. Gin
½ oz. Tequila

Pour Tabasco Sauce into a
shooter glass. Shake
remaining ingredients with ice
and slowly strain onto the
Tabasco. Top with a pinch of
ground cayenne pepper.

Placenta
½ oz. Amaretto
½ oz. Baileys Irish Cream
3 Drops Grenadine

Layer ingredients in order
given in a shot glass.

Plank Walker
1 oz. Amaretto
1 oz. Captain Morgan Spiced
Rum
¼ oz. Dark Creme de Cacao

Layer ingredients in order
given in a shooter glass.

Plaza Suite
1 oz. Black Raspberry
Liqueur
1 oz. Triple Sec

Stir both ingredients with ice
and strain into a sugar-rimmed
shooter glass.

PMS
½ oz. Tequila
½ oz. Tabasco Sauce

Combine both ingredients in a
shot glass.

Poisoned Apple
1 ¼ oz. Sour Apple Pucker
Schnapps
1 ¼ oz. Yukon Jack

Shake both ingredients with
ice and strain into a shooter
glass.

Polar Bear
1 oz. Creme de Banana
1 oz. Peppermint Schnapps
1 oz. Cream

Shake all ingredients with ice
and strain into a shooter glass.

Polish Butterfly
1 oz. Grain Alcohol
1 oz. Blue Curacao
½ oz. Grenadine

Layer ingredients in order
given in a shooter glass.

Polish Kielbasa
1 oz. Vodka
1 oz. Pickle Juice

Shake both ingredients with
ice and strain into a shooter
glass. Garnish with a pickle
spear.

Poof Puss
1 ¼ oz. Wild Turkey 101
1 ¼ oz. Amaretto

Shake both ingredients with
ice and strain into a shooter
glass.

Poop Teeth
1 ½ oz. Bombay Sapphire Gin
1 ½ oz. Kahlua
1 tbs. Grated Parmesan
Cheese

Shake first two ingredients
with ice and strain into a
shooter glass. Stir in the
Parmesan cheese.

Popper
1 ½ oz. Tequila
1 ½ oz. 7-Up

Combine both ingredients in a
shooter glass.

Prairie Chicken
¾ oz. Tequila
1 raw Egg
1 tsp. Tabasco Sauce

Break egg into the bottom of a
large shot glass. Fill with
tequila, then add Tabasco
Sauce.

Prairie Fire
1 oz. Cinnamon Schnapps
1 oz. Absolut Peppar Vodka
2 Dashes Tabasco Sauce

Shake all ingredients with ice
and strain into a shooter glass.

Prairie Oyster
1 ¼ oz. Absolut Vodka
2 oz. Tomato Juice
Dash of Worcestershire Sauce

Shake all ingredients with ice
and strain into a shooter glass.
Drop an unbroken egg yolk
into the drink. Add salt and
pepper to taste.

Premature Ejaculation
1 oz. White Creme de Menthe
1 oz. Baileys Irish Cream
1 oz. Licor 43

Shake all ingredients with ice
and strain into a shooter glass.

Princess
1 ½ oz. Apricot Brandy
½ oz. Cream

Layer ingredients in order
given in a shooter glass.

Puff
1 oz. Tequila
1 oz. Anisette

Shake both ingredients with
ice and strain into a shooter
glass.

Purple Cadillac
1 ¼ oz. Blue Curacao
1 oz. Lime Juice
Dash of Grenadine

Shake all ingredients with ice
and strain into a shooter glass.

Purple Dinosaur
1 oz. Vodka
1 oz. Blue Curacao
½ oz. Orange Juice
½ oz. Cranberry Juice

Shake all ingredients with ice
and strain into a shooter glass.
Float ½ oz. Wilderberry
Schnapps on top.

Purple Drop
½ oz. Parfait Amour
1 oz. Baileys Irish Cream
½ oz. Cointreau
1 ½ oz. Cream

Pour Parfait Amour into a
shooter glass. Shake
remaining ingredients with ice
and slowly strain into the
center of the Parfait Amour.

Purple Fuck
1 oz. White Sambuca
1 oz. Tequila

Pour sambuca into a shooter
glass. Drink sambuca with a
straw as you slowly pour in
the tequila.

Purple Haze
½ oz. Vodka
½ oz. Bacardi 151 Rum
½ oz. Wilderberry Schnapps
½ oz. Blue Curacao
½ oz. Grenadine
½ oz. Pineapple Juice

Shake all ingredients with ice
and strain into a shooter glass.

Purple Helmeted Warrior
½ oz. Blue Curacao
½ oz. Peach Schnapps
½ oz. Gin
½ oz. Southern Comfort
½ oz. Lime Juice
½ oz. Grenadine
Splash of 7-Up

Shake all ingredients with ice
and strain into a shooter glass.

Purple Hooter
1 ½ oz. Absolut Citron Vodka
½ oz. Triple Sec
½ oz. Chambord

Shake all ingredients with ice
and strain into a shooter glass.

Purple Jesus
1 oz. Vodka
1 oz. Grain Alcohol
1 oz. Grape Juice
1 oz. Ginger Ale

Shake all ingredients with ice
and strain into a shooter glass.

Purple Mambo
1 oz. Parfait Amour
1 oz. Anisette

Shake both ingredients with
ice and strain into a shooter
glass.

Purple Mask
1 oz. Vodka
1 oz. Grape Juice
½ oz. Light Creme de Cacao

Shake all ingredients with ice
and strain into a shooter glass.

Purple Moon
1 oz. Vodka
½ oz. Triple Sec
½ oz. Blue Curacao
Splash of Cranberry Juice
Dash of Lime Juice

Shake all ingredients with ice
and strain into a shooter glass.

Purple Mother Fucker
½ oz. Amaretto
½ oz. Blackberry Brandy
½ oz. Southern Comfort
½ oz. Sloe Gin
½ oz. Blue Curacao
½ oz. Orange Juice

Shake all ingredients with ice
and strain into a shooter glass.

Purple Passion
1 ½ oz. Everclear
2 oz. Grape Kool Aid

Shake both ingredients with
ice and strain into a shooter
glass.

Purple People Eater
¾ oz. After Shock Cinnamon
Liqueur
¾ oz. Vodka
1 oz. Minute Maid Blueberry
Soda

Combine all ingredients in a
shooter glass. Top with a
pinch of sugar.

Purple Rain
1 oz. Grain Alcohol
1 oz. Grape Juice
1 oz. Pineapple Juice

Shake all ingredients with ice
and strain into a shooter glass.

Pussy Juice
1 oz. Everclear
1 oz. Captain Morgan Spiced
Rum
1 oz. Cream

Shake all ingredients with ice
and strain into a shooter glass.

Quaalude
1 oz. Vodka
1 oz. Frangelico
1 oz. Cream

Shake all ingredients with ice
and strain into a shooter glass.

Queen Anne
1 oz. Amaretto
1 oz. Frangelico
¼ oz. Bacardi 151 Rum

Layer ingredients in order
given in a shooter glass.
Ignite with a match.

Quick Fuck
¾ oz. Kahlua
¾ oz. Midori Melon Liqueur
¾ oz. Baileys Irish Cream

Layer ingredients in order
given in a shooter glass.

Quicksilver
1 oz. Light Creme de Cacao
1 oz. Peppermint Schnapps
1 oz. Tequila

Shake all ingredients with ice
and strain into a shooter glass.

Rabbit Punch
½ oz. Campari
½ oz. Dark Creme de Cacao
½ oz. Malibu Rum
¾ oz. Baileys Irish Cream

Layer ingredients in order
given in a shooter glass.

Rabbit Stew
1 oz. Peppermint Schnapps
1 oz. Southern Comfort

Shake both ingredients with
ice and strain into a shooter
glass.

Rabid Pitbull
1 ¼ oz. Jack Daniel's
1 oz. Beer
1 oz. 7-Up
3 Dashes Bitters

Shake all ingredients with ice
and strain into a shooter glass.

Race War
¾ oz. Kahlua
¾ oz. Baileys Irish Cream
¾ oz. Stolichnaya Vodka

Layer ingredients in order
given in a shooter glass.

Radioactive Kamikaze
1 oz. Light Rum
1 oz. Malibu Rum
½ oz. Bacardi 151 Rum
½ oz. Blue Curacao
½ oz. Sour Mix

Shake all ingredients with ice
and strain into a shooter glass.

Radioactive Lemonade
1 oz. Vodka
1 oz. Amaretto
1 oz. Lemonade

Shake all ingredients with ice
and strain into a shooter glass.
Float ½ oz. Wilderberry
Schnapps on top.

Rag Pussy
¾ oz. Malibu Rum
¾ oz. Razzmatazz
Dash of Goldschlager
Splash of 7-Up
Splash of Cranberry Juice

Shake all ingredients with ice
and strain into a shooter glass.

Raider
1 oz. Drambuie
1 oz. Baileys Irish Cream
1 oz. Grand Marnier

Layer ingredients in order
given in a shooter glass.

Rainstorm
1 oz. Vodka
1 oz. Blue Curacao
1 oz. Lemonade

Shake all ingredients with ice
and strain into a shooter glass.
Top with a splash of cola.

Rapist
2 oz. Vodka
1 Frozen Popsicle

Crush up popsicle into a
shooter glass. Pour in vodka.
Stir with the popsicle stick.

Raspberry Chill
1 oz. Vodka
1 oz. Raspberry Schnapps
½ oz. Lemonade
½ oz. Pineapple Juice

Shake all ingredients with ice
and strain into a shooter glass.

Raspberry Cooler
1 oz. Vodka
1 oz. Raspberry Schnapps
½ oz. Orange Juice
½ oz. 7-Up

Shake all ingredients with ice
and strain into a shooter glass.

Raspberry Delight
1 oz. Chambord
1 oz. Blackberry Brandy
1 oz. Orange Juice

Shake all ingredients with ice
and strain into a shooter glass.
Top with a splash of club
soda.

Raspberry Grenade
½ oz. Chambord
½ oz. Peach Schnapps
½ oz. Vodka
½ oz. Lime Juice

Shake all ingredients with ice
and strain into a shooter glass.

Raspberry Kamikaze
1 ½ oz. Raspberry Schnapps
1 oz. Triple Sec
½ oz. Lime Juice

Shake all ingredients with ice
and strain into a shooter glass.

Raspberry Lemondrop
1 oz. Raspberry Schnapps
1 oz. Vodka
1 oz. Lemonade

Shake all ingredients with ice
and strain into a shooter glass.

Raspberry Limedrop
1 oz. Raspberry Schnapps
1 oz. Vodka
1 oz. Limeade

Shake all ingredients with ice
and strain into a shooter glass.

Raspberry Sherbet
1 ½ oz. Chambord
½ oz. Triple Sec
½ oz. Canadian Whisky
½ oz. Orange Juice
½ oz. Cream

Shake all ingredients with ice
and strain into a shooter glass.

Raspberry Shortcake
1 ½ oz. Chambord
½ oz. Baileys Irish Cream

Layer ingredients in order
given in a shooter glass.

Rat Piss
1 oz. Vodka
1 oz. Whiskey
1 oz. Mountain Dew

Shake all ingredients with ice
and strain into a shooter glass.

Rattlesnake
1 oz. Kahlua
1 oz. Light Creme de Cacao
1 oz. Baileys Irish Cream

Layer ingredients in order
given in a shooter glass.

Raven's Football
1 oz. Chambord
1 oz. Creme de Banana

Layer ingredients in order
given in a shooter glass.

Rebel Yell
¾ oz. Southern Comfort
¾ oz. Peach Schnapps
1 ½ oz. Orange Juice

Shake all ingredients with ice
and strain into a shooter glass.
Top with a splash of cola.

Red Death
¼ oz. Vodka
¼ oz. Sloe Gin
¼ oz. Southern Comfort
¼ oz. Amaretto
¼ oz. Triple Sec
¼ oz. Lime Juice
¼ oz. Orange Juice
¼ oz. Sour Mix
¼ oz. Grenadine

Shake all ingredients with ice
and strain into a shooter glass.

Red Headed Slut
1 oz. Jägermeister
1 oz. Vodka
Splash of Cranberry Juice

Shake all ingredients with ice
and strain into a shooter glass.

Red Hot
1 ½ oz. Cinnamon Schnapps
2 Dashes Tabasco Sauce

Shake both ingredients with
ice and strain into a shooter
glass.

Red Hot Lover
1 ½ oz. Red Hot Schnapps
1 oz. Orange Juice
1 oz. Cranberry Juice

Shake all ingredients with ice
and strain into a shooter glass.

Red Jobber
1 oz. Malibu Rum
½ oz. Creme de Banana
½ oz. Strawberry Schnapps
½ oz. Jägermeister
Dash of Grenadine

Shake all ingredients with ice
and strain into a shooter glass.

Red October
1 oz. Stolichnaya Vodka
½ oz. Midori Melon Liqueur
½ oz. Sloe Gin
½ oz. Orange Juice
Splash of Sour Mix

Shake all ingredients with ice
and strain into a shooter glass.

Red Raider
1 oz. Bourbon
½ oz. Triple Sec
1 oz. Sour Mix
Dash of Grenadine

Shake all ingredients with ice
and strain into a shooter glass.

Red Royal
1 oz. Crown Royal
1 oz. Amaretto
1 oz. Cranberry Juice

Shake all ingredients with ice
and strain into a shooter glass.

Red Silk Panties
1 oz. Stolichnaya Vodka
½ oz. Peach Schnapps
1 oz. Cranberry Juice

Shake all ingredients with ice
and strain into a shooter glass.

Redneck Shot
1 oz. Cuervo Gold Tequila
1 oz. Hot Damn Cinnamon
Schnapps
1 oz. Wild Turkey

Shake all ingredients with ice
and strain into a shooter glass.

Reese's Cup
1 oz. Light Creme de Cacao
1 oz. Baileys Irish Cream

Layer ingredients in order
given in a shooter glass.
Float 1 unsalted peanut on
top.

Rich Creamy Butter
1 oz. Vodka
1 oz. Melted Butter

Combine both ingredients in a
shooter glass.

Rigor Mortis
1 oz. Kahlua
1 oz. Baileys Irish Cream
1 oz. Bourbon

Shake all ingredients with ice
and strain into a shooter glass.

Rim Job
¾ oz. Light Creme de Cacao
¾ oz. Creme de Banana
¾ oz. Baileys Irish Cream
¾ oz. Wild Turkey

Layer ingredients in order
given in a cherry juice/sugar-
rimmed shooter glass.

Road Kill
¾ oz. Irish Whiskey
¾ oz. Wild Turkey
¾ oz. Bacardi 151 Rum

Shake all ingredients with ice
and strain into a shooter glass.

Road Runner
1 ½ oz. Tia Maria
1 ½ oz. Grand Marnier

Stir both ingredients with ice
and strain into a shooter glass.

Roasted Toasted Almond
1 oz. Grand Marnier
1 oz. Kahlua
1 oz. Baileys Irish Cream

Shake all ingredients with ice
and strain into a shooter glass.

Robin's Nest
1 ½ oz. Gin
½ oz. Apricot Brandy
1 oz. Sour Mix

Shake all ingredients with ice
and strain into a shooter glass.

Robitussin
1 ½ oz. Southern Comfort
1 ½ oz. Amaretto
Dash of Grenadine

Shake all ingredients with ice
and strain into a shooter glass.

Rock Lobster
¾ oz. Light Creme de Cacao
¾ oz. Baileys Irish Cream
½ oz. Amaretto

Layer ingredients in order
given in a shooter glass.
Top with a sprinkle of ground
cinnamon.

Rock Star
¾ oz. Cinnamon Schnapps
¾ oz. Sloe Gin
¾ oz. Triple Sec
¾ oz. Jägermeister

Shake all ingredients with ice
and strain into a shooter glass.
Float ¼ oz. Bacardi 151 Rum
on top. Light with a match.

Rocket Fuel
1 oz. Rumple Minze
1 oz. Bacardi 151 Rum

Combine both ingredients in a
shooter glass.

Rocket Fuel with a Booster
¾ oz. Firewater Cinnamon
Schnapps
¾ oz. Bacardi 151 Rum
¾ oz. Goldschlager

Combine all ingredients in a
shooter glass.

Rocket Launcher
1 oz. Gosling's Bermuda
Black Rum
1 oz. Malibu Rum

Shake both ingredients with
ice and strain into a shooter
glass. Float ¼ oz. Galliano on
top.

Rocky Mountain
1 oz. Southern Comfort
1 oz. Amaretto
½ oz. Lime Juice

Shake all ingredients with ice
and strain into a shooter glass.

Rocky Mountain Bear Fuck
½ oz. Blue Curacao
½ oz. Melon Liqueur
Dash of Canadian Club Rye

Combine all ingredients in a
shot glass.

**Rocky Mountain Beer
Fucker**
¾ oz. Jack Daniel's
¾ oz. Southern Comfort
¾ oz. Tequila

Layer ingredients in order
given in a shooter glass.

Rocky Mountain Mo Fo
¾ oz. Yukon Jack
¾ oz. Amaretto
¾ oz. Lime Juice

Shake all ingredients with ice
and strain into a shooter glass.

**Rocky Mountain Mother
Fucker**
1 ½ oz. Southern Comfort
¾ oz. Amaretto
Dash of Lime Juice

Shake all ingredients with ice
and strain into a shooter glass.

Romeo & Juliet
1 ¼ oz. Goldschlager
½ oz. Stoli Razberi Vodka

Layer ingredients in order
given in a shooter glass.

Romona Banana
1 oz. Creme de Banana
1 oz. Amaretto
1 oz. Peppermint Schnapps

Shake all ingredients with ice
and strain into a shooter glass.

Romulan Ale
1 oz. Bacardi 151 Rum
1 oz. Blue Curacao

Shake both ingredients with
ice and strain into a shooter
glass.

Romulan Dream
1 oz. Grand Marnier
1 oz. Blue Curacao
1 oz. Sour Mix

Shake all ingredients with ice
and strain into a shooter glass.

Root Beer Float
¾ oz. Root Beer Schnapps
½ oz. Stolichnaya Vodka
1 oz. Cream
Splash of Cola

Shake all ingredients with ice
and strain into a shooter glass.

Root Canal
¾ oz. Root Beer Schnapps
¾ oz. Nassau Royale Liqueur

Shake both ingredients with
ice and strain into a shooter
glass.

Rootabuca
1 oz. Root Beer Schnapps
1 oz. White Sambuca

Shake both ingredients with
ice and strain into a shooter
glass.

Rot Gut
1 oz. Hot Damn Cinnamon
Schnapps
1 oz. Vodka

Shake both ingredients with
ice and strain into a shooter
glass.

Rotten Peach
1 ¼ oz. Jack Daniel's
¾ oz. Peach Schnapps

Shake both ingredients with
ice and strain into a shooter
glass.

Rottweiler
½ oz. Tequila
½ oz. Stroh Rum 80
Dash of Tabasco Sauce

Combine all ingredients in a
shot glass.

Royal Caribbean Fuck
¾ oz. Crown Royal
¾ oz. Amaretto
¾ oz. Chambord
Splash of Pineapple Juice
Splash of Cranberry Juice

Shake all ingredients with ice
and strain into a shooter glass.

Royal Chill
2 oz. Crown Royal
¼ oz. Amaretto
1 oz. Cream

Shake all ingredients with ice
and strain into a shooter glass.

Royal Fuck
½ oz. Crown Royal
1 ½ oz. Sour Apple Pucker
Schnapps

Layer ingredients in order
given in a shooter glass.

Royal Schnapreme
2 oz. Crown Royal
1 oz. Peppermint Schnapps

Shake both ingredients with
ice and strain into a shooter
glass.

Rubenstein
½ oz. Vodka
½ oz. Gin
½ oz. Orange Juice
½ oz. Cranberry Juice
½ oz. Tonic Water

Shake all ingredients with ice
and strain into a shooter glass.

Rum & Roses
1 oz. Rum
½ oz. Grenadine
½ oz. Lime Juice

Shake all ingredients with ice
and strain into a shooter glass.

Rumpleschlager
1 ½ oz. Rumple Minze
1 ½ oz. Goldschlager

Stir both ingredients with ice
and strain into a shooter glass.

Runyan
1 oz. Vodka
1 oz. Chambord
½ oz. Sour Mix

Shake all ingredients with ice
and strain into a shooter glass.

Rush Hour
1 oz. Kahlua
1 oz. White Sambuca
1 oz. Baileys Irish Cream

Shake all ingredients with ice
and strain into a shooter glass.

Russian Bell
1 oz. Vodka
1 oz. Baileys Irish Cream
1 oz. Absinthe

Layer ingredients in order
given in a shooter glass.
Ignite with a match.

Russian Bullet
1 ¼ oz. Stolichnaya Vodka
½ oz. White Sambuca
Dash of Tabasco Sauce

Shake all ingredients with ice
and strain into a shooter glass.

Russian Cold Killer
1 ½ oz. Vodka
1 ½ oz. Chambord

Shake both ingredients with
ice and strain into a shooter
glass.

Russian Fire
1 ½ oz. Hot Damn Cinnamon
Schnapps
1 ½ oz. 100 Proof Vodka

Layer ingredients in order
given in a shooter glass.

Russian Kamikaze
3 oz. Vodka
Dash of Chambord

Shake both ingredients with
ice and strain into a shooter
glass.

Russian Quaalude
1 oz. Vodka
½ oz. Kahlua
½ oz. Baileys Irish Cream
½ oz. Frangelico

Shake all ingredients with ice
and strain into a shooter glass.

S.O.B.
¾ oz. Vodka
½ oz. Tia Maria
¼ oz. Chambord
Splash of Pineapple Juice

Shake all ingredients with ice
and strain into a shooter glass.

Saddam Hussein
1 oz. Gosling's Bermuda
Black Rum
1 oz. Malibu Rum

Shake both ingredients with
ice and strain into a shooter
glass. Float ¼ oz. Galliano on
top.

Saikkosen
1 oz. Tia Maria
1 oz. Creme de Cassis
1 oz. Cointreau

Layer ingredients in order
given in a shooter glass.

Salmon Run
1 oz. Cuervo Gold Tequila
1 oz. Tomato Juice
1 oz. Orange Juice

Pour each ingredient into
separate shot glasses.

Sambuca Slide
1 oz. White Sambuca
1 oz. Vodka
1 oz. Cream

Shake all ingredients with ice
and strain into a shooter glass.

Sand Hill Hooker
1 ½ oz. Tequila
1 ½ oz. Pickle Juice

Pour each ingredient into a
separate shooter glass. Drink
together.

Santa Claus is Coming
¾ oz. Cinnamon Schnapps
¾ oz. Melon Liqueur
¾ oz. Rumple Minze

Layer ingredients in order
given in a shooter glass.
Top with whipped cream.

Satan's Mouthwash
1 oz. Jack Daniel's
1 oz. Black Sambuca

Stir both ingredients with ice
and strain into a shooter glass.

Satan's Piss
1 ½ oz. Bacardi 151 Rum
½ oz. Tabasco Sauce

Combine both ingredients in a
shooter glass.

Saveloze
1 oz. Tequila
1 oz. Jägermeister
½ oz. Amaretto
½ oz. Frangelico

Shake all ingredients with ice
and strain into a shooter glass.

Savoy Hotel
½ oz. Light Creme de Cacao
½ oz. Benedictine
½ oz. Brandy

Layer ingredients in order
given in a shooter glass.

Scat
1 oz. Southern Comfort
1 oz. Amaretto
1 oz. Cranberry Juice
Dash of Triple Sec

Shake all ingredients with ice
and strain into a shooter glass.

Scooby Snack
1 oz. Midori Melon Liqueur
1 oz. Malibu Rum

Shake both ingredients with
ice and strain into a shooter
glass. Top with a splash of
pineapple juice and a dash of
whipped cream.

Scooter
1 oz. Amaretto
1 oz. Brandy
1 oz. Cream

Shake all ingredients with ice
and strain into a shooter glass.

Scope
1 oz. Green Creme de Menthe
¾ oz. Dry Vermouth
¾ oz. Cherry Brandy

Shake all ingredients with ice
and strain into a shooter glass.

Scorpion
1 ½ oz. Vodka
1 ½ oz. Blackberry Brandy

Shake both ingredients with
ice and strain into a shooter
glass.

Scorpion Shot
1 oz. Tequila
1 oz. Triple Sec
1 oz. Sour Mix
Dash of Chili Juice

Shake all ingredients with ice
and strain into a shooter glass.

Scotty Was Beamed Up
2 oz. Tequila
½ oz. Galliano

Shake both ingredients with
ice and strain into a shooter
glass.

Screamer
½ oz. Gin
½ oz. Light Rum
½ oz. Tequila
½ oz. Triple Sec
½ oz. Vodka

Shake all ingredients with ice
and strain into a shooter glass.

Screaming Chicken
1 oz. Tequila
1 ½ oz. Tabasco Sauce
1 raw Egg

Combine all ingredients in a
shooter glass.

Screaming Cosmonaut
1 ½ oz. Vodka
1 tbs. Tang Orange Powder

Shake both ingredients with
ice and strain into a shooter
glass.

**Screaming Dead Nazi
Digging for Gold**
1 oz. Jägermeister
1 oz. Rumple Minze
1 oz. Yellow Chartreuse
½ oz. Grain Alcohol

Shake all ingredients with ice
and strain into a shooter glass.

Screaming Golden Nazi
1 oz. Rumple Minze
1 oz. Jägermeister
1 oz. Goldschlager

Layer ingredients in order
given in a shooter glass.

Screaming Green Monster
½ oz. Malibu Rum
½ oz. Bacardi 151 Rum
½ oz. Melon Liqueur
½ oz. Pineapple Juice
½ oz. 7-Up

Shake all ingredients with ice
and strain into a shooter glass.

Screaming Hooker
½ oz. Vodka
½ oz. Creme de Banana
½ oz. Peach Schnapps
½ oz. Cranberry Juice
½ oz. Orange Juice

Shake all ingredients with ice
and strain into a shooter glass.
Top with a splash of ginger
ale.

Screaming Lizard
1 oz. Tequila
1 oz. Green Chartreuse

Layer ingredients in order
given in a shooter glass.
Light with a match.

Screaming Multiple Orgasm
½ oz. Galliano
½ oz. Cointreau
½ oz. Baileys Irish Cream
½ oz. Cream

Shake all ingredients with ice
and strain into a shooter glass.

Screaming Nazi
1 ½ oz. Jägermeister
1 ½ oz. Rumple Minze

Shake both ingredients with
ice and strain into a shooter
glass.

Screaming Orgasm
¾ oz. Vodka
¾ oz. Kahlua
¾ oz. Amaretto
¾ oz. Baileys Irish Cream

Shake all ingredients with ice
and strain into a shooter glass.

Screaming White Orgasm
1 oz. Baileys Irish Cream
½ oz. Kahlua
½ oz. Light Rum
¼ oz. Cointreau
Dash of Cream

Shake all ingredients with ice
and strain into a shooter glass.

Sea Monkey
1 ½ oz. Goldschlager
½ oz. Blue Curacao

Layer ingredients in order
given in a shooter glass.

Sex
1 ½ oz. Kahlua
1 ½ oz. Grand Marnier

Shake both ingredients with
ice and strain into a shooter
glass.

Sex & Candy
1 ½ oz. Peach Schnapps
1 ½ oz. Surge Soda

Stir both ingredients with ice
and strain into a shooter glass.

Sex at My House
¾ oz. Amaretto
¾ oz. Chambord
1 oz. Pineapple Juice

Shake all ingredients with ice
and strain into a shooter glass.

Sex in a Bubblegum Factory
½ oz. Creme de Banana
½ oz. Blue Curacao
½ oz. Apricot Brandy
½ oz. Rum
½ oz. 7-Up

Shake all ingredients with ice
and strain into a shooter glass.

Sex Machine
1 ¼ oz. Kahlua
1 ¼ oz. Baileys Irish Cream
¼ oz. Cream

Shake all ingredients with ice
and strain into a shooter glass.

Sex on a Pink Elephant
½ oz. Peach Schnapps
½ oz. Melon Liqueur
½ oz. Strawberry Liqueur
½ oz. Vodka
½ oz. Cream

Shake all ingredients with ice
and strain into a shooter glass.

Sex on Acid
1 oz. Jägermeister
½ oz. Midori Melon Liqueur
½ oz. Raspberry Liqueur
½ oz. Pineapple Juice
¼ oz. Cranberry Juice

Shake all ingredients with ice
and strain into a shooter glass.

Sex on an Elephant
1 oz. Pear Liqueur
1 oz. Amarula Liqueur

Layer ingredients in order
given in a shooter glass.

Sex on the Bayou
¾ oz. Southern Comfort
¾ oz. Chambord
¾ oz. Pineapple Juice
¾ oz. Orange Juice

Shake all ingredients with ice
and strain into a shooter glass.

Sex on the Beach
¾ oz. Melon Liqueur
¾ oz. Rum
¾ oz. Pineapple Juice
¾ oz. Chambord

Shake all ingredients with ice
and strain into a shooter glass.

Sex on the Beach in Winter
½ oz. Peach Schnapps
½ oz. Vodka
1 oz. Pineapple Juice
1 oz. Cranberry Juice
Dash of Coco Lopez

Shake all ingredients with ice
and strain into a shooter glass.

**Sex on the Beach North Pole
Style**
½ oz. Vodka
½ oz. Chambord
½ oz. Peppermint Schnapps
1 oz. Cranberry Juice

Shake all ingredients with ice
and strain into a shooter glass.

**Sex on the Beach with a
Friend**
¾ oz. Vodka
¾ oz. Midori Melon Liqueur
¾ oz. Creme de Cassis
¾ oz. Pineapple Juice

Shake all ingredients with ice
and strain into a shooter glass.

Sex on the Lake
¾ oz. Creme de Banana
¾ oz. Dark Creme de Cacao
¼ oz. Light Rum
½ oz. Cream

Shake all ingredients with ice
and strain into a shooter glass.

Sex on the Mountain
½ oz. Absolut Vodka
½ oz. Light Blue PowerAde
Whipped Cream

Squirt a dash of whipped
cream into the bottom of a
shooter glass. Shake vodka
and PowerAde with ice and
strain onto whipped cream.
Top with another dash of
whipped cream.

Sex on the Pool Table
½ oz. Blueberry Schnapps
½ oz. Melon Liqueur
½ oz. Vodka
½ oz. Orange Juice
½ oz. Pineapple Juice

Shake all ingredients with ice
and strain into a shooter glass.

Sex on the Rag
1 ½ oz. Baileys Irish Cream
1 ½ oz. Red Cream Soda

Stir both ingredients with ice
and strain into a shooter glass.

Sex on the Sidewalk
¾ oz. Chambord
¾ oz. Melon Liqueur
¾ oz. Cranberry Juice

Shake all ingredients with ice
and strain into a shooter glass.

Sex Up Against the Wall
¾ oz. Vodka
¾ oz. Pineapple Juice
¾ oz. Cranberry Juice
¾ oz. Sour Mix

Shake all ingredients with ice
and strain into a shooter glass.

Sex with a Porcupine
½ oz. Gin
½ oz. Vodka
½ oz. Whiskey
½ oz. Tequila
½ oz. Tabasco Sauce

Shake all ingredients with ice
and strain into a shooter glass.

Sex with an Alligator
¾ oz. Midori Melon Liqueur
¾ oz. Chambord
¼ oz. Jägermeister
¼ oz. Sour Mix

Pour Chambord into a shooter glass. Shake Midori and sour mix with ice and slowly strain on to the Chambord. Layer Jägermeister on top.

Sex with the Captain
½ oz. Captain Morgan Spiced Rum
½ oz. Amaretto
½ oz. Peach Schnapps
Splash of Cranberry Juice
Splash of Orange Juice

Shake all ingredients with ice and strain into a shooter glass.

Sexual Chocolate
1 oz. Dark Creme de Cacao
¾ oz. Vodka
¼ oz. Tia Maria
Dash of Whipped Cream

Shake all ingredients with ice and strain into a shooter glass.

Shanghai
1 ½ oz. Dark Rum
½ oz. White Sambuca
¼ oz. Sour Mix
¼ oz. Grenadine

Shake all ingredients with ice and strain into a shooter glass.

Shark in the Water
1 oz. Vodka
1 oz. Blue Curacao
1 oz. Lemonade

Shake all ingredients with ice and strain into a shooter glass. Float ½ oz. strawberry schnapps on top.

Shavetail
1 oz. Peppermint Schnapps
1 oz. Pineapple Juice
1 oz. Cream

Shake all ingredients with ice and strain into a shooter glass.

Shillelagh
1 ¼ oz. Baileys Irish Cream
½ oz. Jameson Irish Whiskey

Layer ingredients in order given in a shooter glass.

Shit Kicker
¾ oz. Grenadine
¾ oz. Rye Whiskey
¾ oz. Green Creme de Menthe

Layer ingredients in order given in a shooter glass.

Shit on the Grass
1 oz. Midori Melon Liqueur
½ oz. Baileys Irish Cream

Layer ingredients in order given in a shooter glass.

Shit on the Water
1 ½ oz. Blue Curacao
Dash of Baileys Irish Cream

Layer ingredients in order given in a shooter glass.

Shucky Ducky
1 oz. Apricot Brandy
1 oz. White Sambuca

Shake both ingredients with ice and strain into a shooter glass.

Silk Panties
1 ½ oz. Vodka
1 ½ oz. Peach Schnapps

Stir both ingredients with ice and strain into a shooter glass.

Silver Bullet
1 ½ oz. Peppermint Schnapps
1 ½ oz. Rumple Minze

Shake both ingredients with ice and strain into a shooter glass.

Silver Nipple
½ oz. White Sambuca
½ oz. Vodka
½ oz. Triple Sec

Shake all ingredients with ice and strain into a shooter glass.

Silver Spider
¾ oz. Vodka
¾ oz. Rum
¾ oz. Triple Sec
¾ oz. White Creme de
Menthe

Shake all ingredients with ice
and strain into a shooter glass.

Silver Thread
1 oz. Creme de Banana
1 oz. Peppermint Schnapps
1 oz. Baileys Irish Cream

Shake all ingredients with ice
and strain into a shooter glass.

Simple Fuck
¾ oz. Jägermeister
¾ oz. Rumple Minze
¾ oz. Bacardi 151 Rum

Layer ingredients in order
given in a shooter glass.

Sit on My Face
¾ oz. Kahlua
¾ oz. Baileys Irish Cream
¾ oz. Frangelico

Layer ingredients in order
given in a shooter glass.

Sixty-Nine
1 oz. Southern Comfort
¾ oz. Triple Sec
Splash of Cream

Shake all ingredients with ice
and strain into a shooter glass.

Skid Mark
¾ oz. Kahlua
¾ oz. Jägermeister
¾ oz. Rumple Minze

Shake all ingredients with ice
and strain into a shooter glass.

Skinny Mulligan
1 oz. Creme de Banana
1 oz. Advocaat
1 oz. Sloe Gin

Shake all ingredients with ice
and strain into a shooter glass.

Skittle
½ oz. Vodka
½ oz. Cranberry Juice
½ oz. Sour Mix
¼ oz. Creme de Banana
Dash of Grenadine

Shake all ingredients with ice
and strain into a shooter glass.

Slam Dunk
2 oz. Southern Comfort
1 oz. Cranberry Juice
1 oz. Orange Juice

Shake all ingredients with ice
and strain into a shooter glass.

Slammer
1 oz. Any Liqueur or Liquor
1 oz. 7-Up

Combine both ingredients in a
shooter glass. Cover with a
bar coaster and, while holding
coaster and glass, slam down
on table top.

Slammer Hammer
1 oz. Vodka
¾ oz. Spiced Rum
¾ oz. Baileys Irish Cream

Shake all ingredients with ice
and strain into a shooter glass.

Slap Shot
1 ½ oz. Tequila
1 oz. Grape Kool-Aid
1 oz. Club Soda

Shake all ingredients with ice
and strain into a shooter glass.
Top with a teaspoonful of Pop
Rocks candy.

Slapjack
¾ oz. Yukon Jack
¾ oz. Chambord
¾ oz. 7-Up

Shake all ingredients with ice
and strain into a shooter glass.

Sleazy Sex on the Beach
1 ½ oz. Vodka
1 oz. Grand Marnier
1 oz. Orange Juice
1 oz. Cranberry Juice

Shake all ingredients with ice
and strain into a shooter glass.

Sleeper
1 oz. Galliano
1 oz. Kahlua
1 oz. Tequila

Shake all ingredients with ice
and strain into a shooter glass.

Slider
1 oz. Vodka
1 oz. Tequila
1 oz. Creme de Banana

Shake all ingredients with ice
and strain into a shooter glass.

Slimy Sunrise
1 oz. Grain Alcohol
1 oz. Gatorade

Shake both ingredients with
ice and strain into a shooter
glass.

Slimy Worm
¾ oz. Blueberry Schnapps
½ oz. Brandy
2 oz. Apple Juice

Shake all ingredients with ice
and strain into a shooter glass.
Drop a cherry into the drink.

Slingshot
1 oz. Creme de Cassis
1 oz. Canadian Whisky

Shake both ingredients with
ice and strain into a shooter
glass. Top with a splash of
club soda.

Slip Shot
1 ½ oz. Vodka
1 oz. 7-Up

Shake both ingredients with
ice and strain into a shooter
glass. Top with ¼ oz. lime
juice. Garnish with a lime
wedge.

Slippery Dick
½ oz. Creme de Banana
½ oz. Baileys Irish Cream

Layer ingredients in order
given in a shot glass.

Slippery Nipple
1 ½ oz. White Sambuca
½ oz. Baileys Irish Cream

Chill sambuca with ice and
strain into a shooter glass.
Float Baileys on top.

Slippery Nuts
1 ½ oz. Butterscotch
Schnapps
1 ½ oz. Kahlua

Shake both ingredients with
ice and strain into a shooter
glass.

Slippery Saddle
1 oz. Rum
½ oz. Tia Maria
1 oz. Pineapple Juice
½ oz. Orange Juice

Shake all ingredients with ice
and strain into a shooter glass.

Slippery Tit
1 oz. Butterscotch Schnapps
1 oz. Baileys Irish Cream
¼ oz. Light Rum

Layer ingredients in order
given in a shooter glass.

Slope Survival Potion
1 oz. Rye Whiskey
1 oz. Rumple Minze

Shake both ingredients with
ice and strain into a shooter
glass.

Sloppy Seconds
¾ oz. Baileys Irish Cream
¾ oz. Amaretto
¾ oz. Cranberry Juice
¾ oz. Peach Schnapps
Whipped Cream

Squirt a dash of whipped
cream into the bottom of a
shooter glass. Shake
remaining ingredients with ice
and slowly strain onto the
whipped cream.

Sloppy Wet Kiss
1 oz. Watermelon Pucker
Schnapps
1 oz. Amaretto
¼ oz. Sour Mix

Shake all ingredients with ice
and strain into a shooter glass.

Slurrrrr
1 ½ oz. Whiskey
1 ½ oz. Brandy

Shake both ingredients with
ice and strain into a shooter
glass.

Smile
1 ½ oz. Midori Melon Liqueur
1 ½ oz. Apple Brandy

Shake both ingredients with
ice and strain into a shooter
glass.

Smurf
1 oz. Blended Whiskey
½ tsp. Blue Kool-Aid Powder

Combine both ingredients in a
large shot glass.

Smurf Berry
1 oz. Blueberry Schnapps
1 oz. Blue Curacao
1 oz. Cream

Shake all ingredients with ice
and strain into a shooter glass.
Garnish with a stemless
cherry.

Smurf Cum
1 ½ oz. Light Rum
½ oz. Light Creme de Cacao
1 oz. Cream

Shake all ingredients with ice
and strain into a shooter glass.
Pour ½ oz. blue curacao into
the center of the drink.

Smurf Piss
1 oz. Light Rum
½ oz. Blueberry Schnapps
½ oz. Blue Curacao
1 oz. Sour Mix
1 oz. 7-Up

Shake all ingredients with ice
and strain into a shooter glass.

Snake Bite
1 ½ oz. Yukon Jack
½ oz. Lime Juice
1 oz. Orange Juice

Shake all ingredients with ice
and strain into a shooter glass.

Snake River Stinger
2 oz. Gold Tequila
¼ oz. Pernod
¼ oz. White Creme de
Menthe

Shake all ingredients with ice
and strain into a shooter glass.

Snapple Shooter
1 oz. Vodka
½ oz. Triple Sec
1 oz. Cranberry Juice
1 oz. Orange Juice

Shake all ingredients with ice
and strain into a shooter glass.

Snapshot
1 oz. Coffee Liqueur
1 oz. White Sambuca

Shake both ingredients with
ice and strain into a shooter
glass.

Sneaker
½ oz. Chambord
½ oz. Melon Liqueur
½ oz. Malibu Rum
½ oz. Bacardi 151 Rum
½ oz. 7-Up
½ oz. Cranberry Juice

Shake all ingredients with ice
and strain into a shooter glass.

Snot Ball
1 oz. Baileys Irish Cream
Dash of Lime Juice

Combine both ingredients in a
shot glass.

Snotty Toddy
1 oz. Midori Melon Liqueur
1 oz. Bacardi 151 Rum
1 oz. Orange Juice

Shake all ingredients with ice
and strain into a shooter glass.

Snow Cap
1 oz. Tequila
1 oz. Baileys Irish Cream

Layer ingredients in order
given in a shooter glass.

Snowball's Chance in Hell
½ oz. Cinnamon Schnapps
½ oz. Rumple Minze

Combine both ingredients in a
shot glass.

Snowshoe
1 ½ oz. Jack Daniel's
1 ½ oz. Peppermint Schnapps

Shake both ingredients with
ice and strain into a shooter
glass.

Solid Gold
1 oz. Goldkenn
1 oz. Amaretto
1 oz. Vodka

Layer ingredients in order
given in a shooter glass.

Son of a Witch
1 oz. Southern Comfort
1 oz. Apple Schnapps

Shake both ingredients with
ice and strain into a shooter
glass.

Soul Kisser
½ oz. Godiva Chocolate
Liqueur
½ oz. Baileys Irish Cream
½ oz. Licor 43

Layer ingredients in order
given in a shooter glass.

Soulbreaker
½ oz. Firewater Cinnamon
Schnapps
½ oz. Ice 101 Peppermint
Schnapps
½ oz. Fire & Ice
½ oz. Tequila
Dash of Tabasco Sauce

Combine all ingredients in a
shooter glass.

Sour Apple
1 oz. Southern Comfort
1 oz. Midori Melon Liqueur
1 oz. Sour Mix
Dash of Lime Juice

Shake all ingredients with ice
and strain into a shooter glass.

Sour Ball
1 oz. Vodka
1 oz. Triple Sec
1 oz. Lemonade
1 oz. Orange Juice

Shake all ingredients with ice
and strain into a shooter glass.

Sour Grapes
1 oz. Chambord
1 oz. Vodka
1 oz. Sour Mix

Shake all ingredients with ice
and strain into a shooter glass.

Sour Pucker
½ oz. Lime Juice
¾ oz. Vodka
¾ oz. Raspberry Sourpuss
Schnapps

Layer ingredients in order
given in a shooter glass.

Sour Puss
1 oz. Vodka
½ oz. Melon Liqueur
¼ oz. Lemon Juice
Dash of Grenadine

Shake all ingredients with ice
and strain into a shooter glass.

Sour Widowmaker
1 ½ oz. Tequila
¾ oz. Lime Juice
1 tsp. Rock Salt

Pour the rock salt into the
bottom of a shooter glass.
Shake tequila and lime juice
with ice and strain into the
glass.

South Beach
1 oz. Raspberry Schnapps
½ oz. Peach Schnapps
½ oz. Vodka
½ oz. Sour Mix
½ oz. Cranberry Juice

Shake all ingredients with ice
and strain into a shooter glass.

**Southern Apple Pie
Slammer**
1 oz. Southern Comfort
2 oz. Apple Juice

Shake both ingredients with
ice and strain into a shooter
glass. Top with a dash of
ground cinnamon.

Southern Blues
1 oz. Bluesberry Schnapps
1 oz. Southern Comfort

Shake both ingredients with
ice and strain into a shooter
glass.

Southern Chase
¾ oz. Jack Daniel's
¾ oz. Southern Comfort
¾ oz. Galliano

Shake all ingredients with ice
and strain into a shooter glass.

**Southern Comfort
Kamikaze**
1 ½ oz. Southern Comfort
1 oz. Triple Sec
½ oz. Lime Juice

Shake all ingredients with ice
and strain into a shooter glass.

Southern Monkey
1 oz. Southern Comfort
1 oz. Kahlua
1 oz. Creme de Banana

Shake all ingredients with ice
and strain into a shooter glass.

Southern Suicide
¾ oz. Jack Daniel's
¾ oz. Southern Comfort
½ oz. Orange Juice
¼ oz. 7-Up
¼ oz. Grenadine

Shake all ingredients with ice
and strain into a shooter glass.

Spanish Dynamite
1 oz. Tequila
¼ oz. Cointreau
½ oz. Licor 43

Combine all ingredients in a
shooter glass. Garnish with a
cinnamon stick.

Sperm Whale
1 oz. Rye Whiskey
1 oz. Southern Comfort
1 oz. Cream

Shake all ingredients with ice
and strain into a shooter glass.

Spermafrost
1 ½ oz. Rumple Minze
Dash of Cream

Shake Rumple Minze with ice
and strain into a shooter glass.
Top with a the dash of cream.

Spiced Apple
1 ½ oz. Sour Apple Pucker
Schnapps
¾ oz. Cinnamon Schnapps

Shake both ingredients with
ice and strain into a shooter
glass.

Spice-N-Berry
1 ½ oz. Captain Morgan
Spiced Rum
1 ½ oz. Black Raspberry
Liqueur

Stir both ingredients with ice
and strain into a shooter glass.

Spicy Middle Eastern Treat
1 oz. Jägermeister
1 oz. Gin

Layer ingredients in order
given in a shooter glass.
Top with a sprinkle of ground
cinnamon.

Spider Bite
1 oz. Anisette
1 oz. Tequila

Shake both ingredients with
ice and strain into a shooter
glass.

Spitting Hamster
¾ oz. Cointreau
¾ oz. Tequila
¾ oz. Triple Sec
Dash of White Sambuca
Dash White Creme de Menthe

Shake all ingredients with ice
and strain into a shooter glass.

Spongehead
1 oz. Amaretto
½ oz. Vodka
½ oz. Grenadine

Shake all ingredients with ice
and strain into a shooter glass.

Springbok
1 oz. Amarula Cream
1 oz. Peppermint Schnapps

Layer ingredients in order
given in a shooter glass.

Spy Catcher
1 oz. Canadian Whisky
½ oz. White Sambuca

Shake both ingredients with
ice and strain into a shooter
glass.

Spy's Demise
½ oz. Vodka
½ oz. Gin
½ oz. Sloe Gin
¼ oz. Rum
¼ oz. Grenadine
½ oz. Sour Mix

Shake all ingredients with ice
and strain into a shooter glass.
Top with a splash of 7-Up.

Squashed Frog
1 oz. Midori Melon Liqueur
1 drop Advocaat
1 drop Cherry Advocaat
¼ oz. Baileys Irish Cream

Layer ingredients in order
given in a shooter glass.

SR-71
1 oz. Amaretto
1 oz. Baileys Irish Cream

Layer ingredients in order
given in a shooter glass.

St. Louis Blues
1 oz. Blue Curacao
1 oz. Vodka
1 oz. Lemonade
1 oz. 7-Up

Shake all ingredients with ice
and strain into a shooter glass.

Stalactite
1 ¼ oz. White Sambuca
½ oz. Baileys Irish Cream
¼ oz. Chambord

Layer first two ingredients in
a shooter glass. Slowly pour
Chambord in the middle of
the drink.

Star Wars
1 oz. Southern Comfort
1 oz. Grand Marnier
1 oz. Pineapple Juice
¼ oz. Grenadine

Shake all ingredients with ice
and strain into a shooter glass.

Starburst
½ oz. Licor 43
½ oz. Black Raspberry
Liqueur
½ oz. Smirnoff Silver Vodka
½ oz. Sour Mix
½ oz. 7-Up

Splash of Cranberry Juice
Shake all ingredients with ice
and strain into a shooter glass.

Starry Night
1 oz. Goldschlager
1 oz. Jägermeister

Layer ingredients in order
given in a shooter glass.

Stars & Stripes
1 oz. Parfait Amour
1 oz. Grand Marnier
1 oz. Gin

Layer ingredients in order
given in a shooter glass.

Stealth Bomber
½ oz. Kahlua
½ oz. Creme de Banana
½ oz. Baileys Irish Cream
½ oz. Grand Marnier

Layer ingredients in order
given in a shooter glass.

Stickler
½ oz. Kahlua
½ oz. Amaretto
½ oz. Baileys Irish Cream
½ oz. Vodka
½ oz. Galliano

Shake all ingredients with ice
and strain into a shooter glass.

Sticky Fingers
¾ oz. Amaretto
¾ oz. Melon Liqueur
¾ oz. Creme de Banana

Layer ingredients in order
given in a shooter glass.

Stiletto
1 oz. Chambord
1 oz. Stolichnaya Vodka

Layer ingredients in order
given in a shooter glass.

Stimulated Clitoris
1 ¼ oz. Bacardi Light Rum
¼ oz. Grenadine
¼ oz. Lime Juice
Dash of Triple Sec
1 tsp. Sugar

Shake all ingredients with ice
and strain into a shooter glass.

Stinger Missile
1 ¼ oz. Courvoisier VS
1 oz. Rumple Minze

Stir both ingredients with ice
and strain into a shooter glass.

Stinger X
1 oz. Vodka
1 oz. After Shock Cinnamon
Liqueur
1 oz. Everclear

Layer ingredients in order
given in a shooter glass.

Stop Light
1 Hawaiian Punch Shooter
1 Boomer Shooter
1 Melon Ball Shooter

Carefully stack each shooter
to resemble a stop light.

Storm Trooper
1 ¼ oz. Jägermeister
1 ¼ oz. Peppermint Schnapps

Shake both ingredients with
ice and strain into a shooter
glass.

Straight Ticket
1 ½ oz. Cuervo Gold Tequila

Chill tequila with ice and
strain into a shooter glass.
Serve with a slice of lime and
a salt shaker.

Strawberry Bomb
¾ oz. Strawberry Schnapps
¼ oz. Grain Alcohol

Combine both ingredients in a
shot glass.

Strawberry Chill
1 oz. Strawberry Schnapps
1 oz. Vodka
½ oz. Lemonade
½ oz. Pineapple Juice

Shake all ingredients with ice
and strain into a shooter glass.

Strawberry Cooler
1 oz. Strawberry Schnapps
1 oz. Vodka
½ oz. Orange Juice
½ oz. 7-Up

Shake all ingredients with ice
and strain into a shooter glass.

Strawberry Kamikaze
1 oz. Strawberry Schnapps
1 oz. Vodka
1 oz. Sour Mix

Shake all ingredients with ice
and strain into a shooter glass.

Strawberry Lemonade
1 oz. Strawberry Schnapps
1 oz. Vodka
1 ½ oz. Lemonade

Shake all ingredients with ice
and strain into a shooter glass.

Strawberry Lemondrop
1 oz. Strawberry Liqueur
1 oz. Vodka
1 oz. Lemonade

Shake all ingredients with ice
and strain into a shooter glass.

Strawberry Limedrop
1 oz. Strawberry Liqueur
1 oz. Vodka
1 oz. Limeade

Shake all ingredients with ice
and strain into a shooter glass.

Strawberry Shortcake
2 oz. Strawberry Liqueur
1 oz. Amaretto

Stir both ingredients with ice
and strain into a shooter glass.
Float ½ oz. cream on top.

Strawberry Shots
1 oz. Chambord
1 oz. Baileys Irish Cream
1 oz. Cream

Shake all ingredients with ice
and strain into a shooter glass.
Float a slice of fresh
strawberry on top.

Strega Nera
1 oz. Black Sambuca
1 oz. Strega

Layer ingredients in order
given in a shooter glass.

Strega Salute
¾ oz. Grenadine
¾ oz. Green Creme de
Menthe
¾ oz. Strega

Layer ingredients in order
given in a shooter glass.

Sublime
¾ oz. Amaretto
¾ oz. Creme de Banana
¾ oz. Light Creme de Cacao

Layer ingredients in order
given in a shooter glass.

Suck Me Harder
½ oz. After Shock Cinnamon
Liqueur
½ oz. Goldschlager
½ oz. Gin
½ oz. Pineapple Juice

Shake all ingredients with ice
and strain into a shooter glass.
Top with a dash of whipped
cream.

Sucker Punch
1 oz. Jack Daniel's
1 oz. Cold Espresso
½ oz. Baileys Irish Cream

Shake first two ingredients
with ice and strain into a
shooter glass. Float Baileys on
top.

Sudden Impact
¾ oz. Jack Daniel's
¾ oz. Tequila
¾ oz. Peppermint Schnapps

Shake all ingredients with ice
and strain into a shooter glass.

Suicide Kings
¾ oz. Jack Daniel's
¾ oz. Johnny Walker Red
¾ oz. Bacardi 151 Rum

Shake all ingredients with ice
and strain into a shooter glass.

Summer Breeze
¾ oz. Southern Comfort
¾ oz. Triple Sec
¼ oz. Sour Mix
¾ oz. Orange Juice
¾ oz. Cranberry Juice

Shake all ingredients with ice
and strain into a shooter glass.

Sun & Surf
¾ oz. Kahlua
¾ oz. Grand Marnier
¾ oz. Tequila

Shake all ingredients with ice
and strain into a shooter glass.

Sundrop
1 oz. Vodka
¼ oz. Pink Lemonade
½ oz. 7-Up
1 tsp. Sugar

Shake all ingredients with ice
and strain into a shooter glass.

Sunny's Halo
¾ oz. Cointreau
¾ oz. Tequila
¾ oz. Amaretto

Shake all ingredients with ice
and strain into a shooter glass.

Sun's Slammer
1 oz. Southern Comfort
1 oz. Strawberry Liqueur
1 oz. Orange Juice

Shake all ingredients with ice
and strain into a shooter glass.

Sunshot
1 oz. Vodka
1 oz. Triple Sec
1 oz. Sunny Delight Orange
Drink

Shake all ingredients with ice
and strain into a shooter glass.

Suntan Lotion
½ oz. Vodka
¾ oz. Malibu Rum
¾ oz. Creme de Banana
1 oz. Pineapple Juice

Shake all ingredients with ice
and strain into a shooter glass.

Surf Rat
1 oz. Tequila
1 oz. Kahlua
1 ½ oz. Cream

Shake all ingredients with ice
and strain into a shooter glass.

Surfer on Acid
1 oz. Jägermeister
1 oz. Malibu Rum
1 oz. Pineapple Juice

Shake all ingredients with ice
and strain into a shooter glass.

Surfer on Acid & Crack
½ oz. Jägermeister
½ oz. Malibu Rum
½ oz. Rumple Minze
½ oz. Bacardi 151 Rum
½ oz. Pineapple Juice
½ oz. 7-Up

Shake all ingredients with ice
and strain into a shooter glass.

Surfer on Acid in Hawaii
¾ oz. Jägermeister
¾ oz. Malibu Rum
½ oz. Chambord
¾ oz. Pineapple Juice
¾ oz. Cranberry Juice

Shake all ingredients with ice
and strain into a shooter glass.

Surfer on Acid in Key West
½ oz. Jägermeister
½ oz. Vodka
½ oz. Melon Liqueur
½ oz. Razzmatazz
½ oz. Cranberry Juice
½ oz. Sour Mix

Shake all ingredients with ice
and strain into a shooter glass.

Swamp Water
1 ½ oz. Rum
½ oz. Blue Curacao
1 oz. Orange Juice
½ oz. Sour Mix

Shake all ingredients with ice
and strain into a shooter glass.

Sweaty Balls
¾ oz. Vodka
¾ oz. Southern Comfort
¾ oz. Everclear
Dash of Lemon Juice

Shake all ingredients with ice
and strain into a shooter glass.
Float 2 shelled peanuts on top.

Sweaty Dead Nazi
¾ oz. Jägermeister
¾ oz. Goldschlager
¾ oz. Inferno

Shake all ingredients with ice
and strain into a shooter glass.

Sweaty Lumberjack
½ oz. Tequila
½ oz. Bacardi 151 Rum
Dash of Tabasco Sauce

Combine all ingredients in a
shot glass.

**Sweaty Mexican
Lumberjack**
1 ¼ oz. Yukon Jack
1 ¼ oz. Tequila
Dash of Tabasco Sauce

Shake all ingredients with ice
and strain into a shooter glass.

**Sweaty Mexican Yeast
Infection**
1 oz. Tequila
½ oz. Wild Turkey
½ oz. Bacardi 151 Rum
Dash of Tabasco Sauce

Shake all ingredients with ice
and strain into a mayonnaise-
rimmed shooter glass.

Swedish Blowjob
¾ oz. Kahlua
¾ oz. Creme de Banana
¾ oz. Baileys Irish Cream

Layer ingredients in order
given in a shooter glass.

Swedish Color
¾ oz. Absolut Vodka
¾ oz. Creme de Banana
¾ oz. Blue Curacao

Layer ingredients in order
given in a shooter glass.

Swedish Fish
¾ oz. Black Haus
¾ oz. Peach Schnapps
¾ oz. Cranberry Juice

Shake all ingredients with ice
and strain into a shooter glass.

Swedish Goldfish
¾ oz. Southern Comfort
¾ oz. Raspberry Schnapps
¾ oz. Blueberry Schnapps
¾ oz. Cranberry Juice

Shake all ingredients with ice
and strain into a shooter glass.

Sweet & Tart
1 ½ oz. Absolut Citron Vodka
Splash of Sour Mix
Splash of 7-Up
1 tsp. Sugar
Twist of Lemon and Lime

Shake all ingredients with ice
and strain into a shooter glass.

Sweet Blood
1 ¼ oz. Vodka
1 ¼ oz. Cranberry Juice

Shake both ingredients with
ice and strain into a shooter
glass.

Sweet Cream
1 ½ oz. Kahlua
½ oz. Baileys Irish Cream

Layer ingredients in order
given in a shooter glass.

Sweet Peach
¾ oz. Peach Schnapps
¾ oz. Amaretto
¾ oz. Orange Juice

Shake all ingredients with ice
and strain into a shooter glass.

Sweet Tart
1 ½ oz. Chambord
1 oz. Sour Mix

Shake both ingredients with
ice and strain into a shooter
glass.

Sweet Tits
1 oz. Strawberry Schnapps
1 oz. Apricot Brandy
Dash of Lemon Juice
Dash of Lime Juice

Shake all ingredients with ice
and strain into a shooter glass.

Sweet Water
¾ oz. Vodka
¾ oz. Triple Sec
½ oz. Light Rum
½ oz. Gin
½ oz. Butterscotch Schnapps

Shake all ingredients with ice
and strain into a shooter glass.

Swell Sex
½ oz. Malibu Rum
½ oz. Melon Liqueur
½ oz. Vodka
½ oz. Pineapple Juice
Splash of Cream

Shake all ingredients with ice
and strain into a shooter glass.

T.K.O.
¾ oz. Tequila
¾ oz. Kahlua
¾ oz. Ouzo

Shake all ingredients with ice
and strain into a shooter glass.

T.N.T.
1 oz. Tequila
Dash of Tabasco Sauce

Combine both ingredients in a
shot glass.

Taffy Apple
1 oz. Sour Apple Pucker
Schnapps
1 oz. Butterscotch Schnapps

Shake both ingredients with
ice and strain into a shooter
glass.

Tahitian Fu-Fu
1 oz. Malibu Rum
1 oz. Tuaca
1 oz. Cranberry Juice
Splash of Orange Juice

Shake all ingredients with ice
and strain into a shooter glass.

Tank
1 ½ oz. Tanqueray Gin
1 ½ oz. Jack Daniel's

Shake both ingredients with
ice and strain into a shooter
glass.

Tarantula Fizzler
1 oz. Vodka
½ oz. Tequila
½ oz. Light Rum
Dash of Tabasco Sauce

Shake all ingredients with ice
and strain into a shooter glass.

Tasty Orgasm
1 ½ oz. Peppermint Schnapps
1 ½ oz. Baileys Irish Cream

Shake both ingredients with
ice and strain into a shooter
glass.

Tawny Kitaen
1 oz. Amaretto
1 oz. Vodka
½ oz. Chocolate Syrup

Shake all ingredients with ice
and strain into a shooter glass.

Tear Drop
1 ¼ oz. Absolut Peppar
Vodka
¼ oz. Grand Marnier

Stir both ingredients with ice
and strain into a shooter glass.
Drop a cherry in the center of
the drink.

Teddy Bear
1 oz. Root Beer Schnapps
1 oz. Vodka

Layer ingredients in order
given in a shooter glass.

Tequila Dairy
1 oz. Tequila
1 oz. Vodka
Splash of Cream

Combine all ingredients in a
shooter glass. Top with a dash
of whipped cream.

Tequila Fire
1 ½ oz. Tequila
3 Dashes Tabasco Sauce

Combine both ingredients in a
shooter glass.

Tequila Headfuck
1 ½ oz. Tequila
1 ½ oz. Baileys Irish Cream

Shake both ingredients with ice and strain into a shooter glass. Drop a cherry in the middle.

Tequila Popper
1 oz. Tequila
½ oz. 7-Up

Combine both ingredients in a shooter glass. Cover glass with a beer coaster and slam down on the table. Drink immediately.

Tequila Slammer
1 oz. Tequila
½ oz. 7-Up

Combine both ingredients in a shooter glass. Cover glass with a beer coaster and slam down on the table. Drink immediately.

Tequila Threat
1 ½ oz. Tequila
½ oz. Blackberry Brandy
1 oz. Triple Sec
½ oz. Lime Juice

Shake all ingredients with ice and strain into a shooter glass.

Terminator
1 ½ oz. Southern Comfort
1 ½ oz. Jägermeister

Shake both ingredients with ice and strain into a shooter glass.

Test Tube Baby
1 oz. Tequila
1 oz. Amaretto

Combine both ingredients in a shooter glass. To the center of the drink, add 1 drop of cream and 1 drop of tomato juice. Don't stir.

Tetanus Shot
1 oz. Peppermint Schnapps
1 oz. Cherry Brandy
1 oz. Baileys Irish Cream

Shake all ingredients with ice and strain into a shooter glass.

Texas Flag
½ oz. After Shock Cinnamon Liqueur
½ oz. Goldschlager
½ oz. Avalanche Blue Peppermint Schnapps

Layer ingredients in order given in a shooter glass.

Texas Snake Bite
1 oz. Tequila
Dash of Tabasco Sauce

Combine both ingredients in a shot glass. Top with a pinch of ground black pepper.

TGV
¾ oz. Tequila
¾ oz. Gin
¾ oz. Vodka

Shake all ingredients with ice and strain into a shooter glass.

Thighs of a German Girl
¾ oz. Jägermeister
¾ oz. Rumple Minze
¾ oz. Chocolate Schnapps

Shake all ingredients with ice and strain into a shooter glass.

Third Reich
¾ oz. Goldschlager
¾ oz. Jägermeister
¾ oz. Rumple Minze

Shake all ingredients with ice and strain into a shooter glass.

Three Wise Men
1 oz. Cuervo Gold Tequila
1 oz. Jack Daniel's
1 oz. Jim Beam

Shake all ingredients with ice and strain into a shooter glass.

Three Wise Men & the Mexican Porter
¾ oz. Jack Daniel's
¾ oz. Jim Beam
¾ oz. Johnny Walker
¾ oz. Cuervo Gold Tequila

Shake all ingredients with ice and strain into a shooter glass.

Three Wise Men & Their Pappy on a Game Hunt
½ oz. Jack Daniel's
½ oz. Jim Beam
½ oz. Johnny Walker
½ oz. Old Grand Dad
½ oz. Wild Turkey

Shake all ingredients with ice and strain into a shooter glass.

**Three Wise Men Over the
Border with a Kick**
½ oz. Jack Daniel's
½ oz. Jim Beam
½ oz. Johnny Walker Black
½ oz. Cuervo Gold Tequila
½ oz. Goldschlager

Shake all ingredients with ice
and strain into a shooter glass.

Three-Legged Monkey
¾ oz. Crown Royal
¾ oz. Seagram's 7
¾ oz. Wild Turkey 101

Shake all ingredients with ice
and strain into a shooter glass.

Thumb in the Ass
½ oz. Butterscotch Schnapps
½ oz. Cinnamon Schnapps
½ oz. Peach Schnapps
½ oz. Peppermint Schnapps
½ oz. Blueberry Schnapps

Shake all ingredients with ice
and strain into a shooter glass.

Tidy Bowl
¾ oz. Vodka
¼ oz. Blue Curacao

Stir both ingredients with ice
and strain into a shot glass.
Drop 2 raisins into the drink.

Tie Me to the Bedpost
½ oz. Malibu Rum
½ oz. Absolut Citron Vodka
½ oz. Melon Liqueur
½ oz. Sour Mix

Shake all ingredients with ice
and strain into a shooter glass.

Tie-Dyed Mind Fuck
½ oz. Blue Curacao
½ oz. Creme de Banana
½ oz. Melon Liqueur
½ oz. Grenadine

Layer ingredients in order
given in a shooter glass.

Tiger Balls
1 oz. Jack Daniel's
1 oz. Grain Alcohol
1 oz. Draft Beer

Shake all ingredients with ice
and strain into a shooter glass.

To the Moon
¾ oz. Kahlua
¾ oz. Amaretto
¾ oz. Baileys Irish Cream
¾ oz. Bacardi 151 Rum

Shake all ingredients with ice
and strain into a shooter glass.

Toffee Apple
¾ oz. Apple Schnapps
½ oz. Butterscotch Schnapps

Shake both ingredients with
ice and strain into a shooter
glass.

Toilet Wrecker
¾ oz. Vodka
¾ oz. Red Hot Schnapps
¾ oz. Tequila
¼ oz. Tabasco Sauce
1 tbs. Horseradish
Pinch of Ground Pepper

Combine all ingredients in a
shooter glass.

Tokyo Tea
½ oz. Vodka
½ oz. Light Rum
½ oz. Gin
½ oz. Triple Sec
½ oz. Midori Melon Liqueur
½ oz. Sour Mix

Shake all ingredients with ice
and strain into a shooter glass.

Tomato Drop
1 ½ oz. Vodka
1 Tomato wedge
Pinch of Salt

Combine all ingredients in a
shooter glass.

Tomato Whip
1 oz. Cherry Whiskey
1 oz. Tomato Juice

Shake both ingredients with
ice and strain into a shooter
glass. Top with a dash of
whipped cream.

Tootsie Roll Extreme
1 oz. Godiva Chocolate
Liqueur
½ oz. Cointreau
1 oz. Orange Juice

Shake all ingredients with ice
and strain into a shooter glass.

Top Banana
1 oz. Vodka
1 oz. Creme de Banana
1 oz. Orange Juice

Shake all ingredients with ice
and strain into a shooter glass.

Towering Inferno
¾ oz. Kahlua
¾ oz. Wild Turkey
¾ oz. Cream
½ oz. Brandy

Layer ingredients in order given in a shooter glass. Ignite with a match.

Toxic Jelly Bean
¾ oz. Ouzo
¾ oz. Jägermeister
½ oz. Blackberry Brandy

Layer ingredients in order given in a shooter glass.

Toyota Crash
2 oz. Southern Comfort
1 oz. Malibu Rum
Splash of 7-Up

Shake all ingredients with ice and strain into a shooter glass.

Traffic Light
1 oz. Creme de Noyeaux
1 oz. Galliano
1 oz. Melon Liqueur

Layer ingredients in order given in a shooter glass.

Traveler's Tales
1 oz. Vodka
1 oz. Maui Tropical Schnapps
½ oz. Lemonade
½ oz. 7-Up

Shake all ingredients with ice and strain into a shooter glass.

Triaminic Cough Syrup
1 ½ oz. Goldschlager
½ oz. Grape Kool-Aid

Shake both ingredients with ice and strain into a shooter glass.

Triple T
¾ oz. Tanqueray Gin
¾ oz. Tequila
¾ oz. Wild Turkey

Shake all ingredients with ice and strain into a shooter glass.

Tropical Burn
1 oz. Malibu Rum
1 oz. Peach Schnapps
Splash of Cranberry Juice
Splash of Pineapple Juice

Shake all ingredients with ice and strain into a shooter glass.

Tropical Paradise
1 ½ oz. Light Rum
½ oz. Creme de Banana
½ oz. Orange Juice
½ oz. Strawberry Juice
Dash of Grenadine

Shake all ingredients with ice and strain into a shooter glass.

Tropical Storm
1 oz. Rum
1 oz. Passion Fruit Liqueur
1 oz. Sour Mix

Shake all ingredients with ice and strain into a shooter glass.

Tropical Tease
1 oz. Pina Colada Schnapps
½ oz. Rum
¼ oz. Grenadine
½ oz. Pineapple Juice

Shake all ingredients with ice and strain into a shooter glass.

Tropico Orgasm
1 oz. Bacardi Tropico Rum
½ oz. Bacardi 151 Rum

Shake both ingredients with ice and strain into a shooter glass.

Turban
1 oz. Tequila
1 oz. Bourbon

Shake both ingredients with ice and strain into a shooter glass.

Turkey Roaster
½ oz. Wild Turkey 101
½ oz. Tia Maria
½ oz. Baileys Irish Cream
½ oz. Cream

Shake all ingredients with ice and strain into a shooter glass.

Turkey Shooter
¾ oz. Wild Turkey 101
¼ oz. White Creme de Menthe

Combine both ingredients in a shot glass.

Turkish Tiger
1 oz. Vodka
½ oz. Condensed Milk

Shake both ingredients with ice and strain into a shooter glass. Top with a sprinkle of ground cinnamon.

Tutti Frutti
1 oz. Melon Liqueur
½ oz. Strawberry Liqueur
½ oz. Creme de Banana
½ oz. Peach Brandy

Shake all ingredients with ice and strain into a shooter glass.

TV Tower
¾ oz. Grenadine
¾ oz. Blue Curacao
¾ oz. Sherry

Layer ingredients in order given in a shooter glass.

TVR
¾ oz. Tequila
¾ oz. Vodka
1 oz. Red Bull Beer

Combine all ingredients in a shooter glass.

Twilight Zone
1 ¼ oz. Vodka
1 ¼ oz. Blue Curacao

Stir both ingredients with ice and strain into a shooter glass. Float a lemon slice on top.

Twisted Bull
¾ oz. Absolut Citron Vodka
2 oz. Beef Broth

Stir both ingredients with ice and strain into a shooter glass. Garnish with a wedge of lime.

Twisted Jack
½ oz. Jack Daniel's
½ oz. Southern Comfort
½ oz. Chambord
½ oz. Amaretto
½ oz. Sour Mix

Shake all ingredients with ice and strain into a shooter glass.

Twister
1 oz. Smirnoff Citrus Twist Vodka
1 ½ oz. Zima Malt Beverage

Shake both ingredients with ice and strain into a shooter glass.

Two Minute Warning
1 oz. Crown Royal
1 oz. Buttershots Schnapps

Layer ingredients in order given in a shooter glass.

Ty-D-Bowl
1 ½ oz. Light Rum
½ oz. Blue Curacao
1 oz. 7-Up

Shake all ingredients with ice and strain into a shooter glass.

Ugly Green Pussy
1 oz. Midori Melon Liqueur
¾ oz. Green Creme de Menthe
¾ oz. Vodka
Splash of Lime Juice

Shake all ingredients with ice and strain into a shooter glass.

Uncontrollable
¾ oz. Grand Marnier
¾ oz. Watermelon Pucker Schnapps
½ oz. Sour Apple Pucker Schnapps
Splash of Cranberry Juice
Splash of Pineapple Juice

Shake all ingredients with ice and strain into a shooter glass.

Under the Boardwalk
1 oz. Vodka
1 oz. Strawberry Liqueur
½ oz. Lemonade
½ oz. Orange Juice

Shake all ingredients with ice and strain into a shooter glass. Float ½ oz. Wilderberry Schnapps on top.

Under Water
1 oz. Peach Schnapps
1 oz. Blue Curacao
1 oz. Baileys Irish Cream

Layer ingredients in order given in a shooter glass.

Undertaker
1 ½ oz. Black Sambuca
½ oz. Baileys Irish Cream

Layer ingredients in order given in a shooter glass.

Unholy Water
½ oz. Captain Morgan Parrot
Bay Rum
½ oz. Smirnoff 100 Proof
Vodka
½ oz. Everclear
½ oz. Gin
½ oz. White Tequila

Shake all ingredients with ice
and strain into a shooter glass.

Universe
1 oz. Vodka
1 oz. Melon Liqueur
1 oz. Pineapple Juice

Shake all ingredients with ice
and strain into a shooter glass.

Unlikely Pirates
¾ oz. Captain Morgan Parrot
Bay Rum
¾ oz. Jack Daniel's
¾ oz. Cuervo Gold Tequila

Layer ingredients in order
given in a shooter glass.

Up Chuck
¾ oz. Jägermeister
¾ oz. Cuervo Gold Tequila
¾ oz. Bacardi 151 Rum

Layer ingredients in order
given in a shooter glass.

Up on the Roof
1 oz. Vodka
1 oz. Cherry Schnapps
1 oz. Lemonade

Shake all ingredients with ice
and strain into a shooter glass.
Top with a splash of cola.

Upper Cut
1 oz. Jack Daniel's
1 oz. Amaretto
1 oz. Orange Juice

Shake all ingredients with ice
and strain into a shooter glass.

Urban Cowboy
1 oz. Southern Comfort
1 oz. Jack Daniel's

Shake both ingredients with
ice and strain into a shooter
glass.

Urine
1 ½ oz. Licor 43
1 oz. Peppermint Schnapps

Shake both ingredients with
ice and strain into a shooter
glass.

Valium
1 oz. Crown Royal
1 oz. Peach Schnapps
1 oz. Cranberry Juice

Shake all ingredients with ice
and strain into a shooter glass.

Vampire Slobber
½ oz. White Sambuca
½ oz. Amaretto
½ oz. Baileys Irish Cream
½ oz. Grenadine

Layer ingredients in order
given in a shooter glass.

Vanilla Ice Cream
1 oz. Light Rum
1 oz. Licor 43
1 oz. Cream

Shake all ingredients with ice
and strain into a shooter glass.

Vegas Blowjob
1 oz. Creme de Banana
½ oz. Light Rum
½ oz. Jägermeister
1 oz. Orange Juice
1 oz. Pineapple Juice

Shake all ingredients with ice
and strain into a shooter glass.

Vibrator
¾ oz. Baileys Irish Cream
1 ½ oz. Southern Comfort

Layer ingredients in order
given in a shooter glass.

Vicks Blue
¾ oz. Green Creme de
Menthe
¾ oz. Blue Curacao
¾ oz. Absolut Citron Vodka

Layer ingredients in order
given in a shooter glass.

Vodka Sundowner
2 oz. Vodka
1 oz. Orange Juice
¼ oz. Raspberry Syrup

Layer ingredients in order
given in a shooter glass.

Volcano
1 ¼ oz. Absolut Peppar
Vodka Dash of Grenadine

Combine both ingredients in a
large shot glass.

Vomiting Frog
1 oz. Vodka
1 oz. Melon Liqueur
¼ oz. Baileys Irish Cream

Layer ingredients in order
given in a shooter glass.

Vulcan Death Grip
1 ½ oz. Ouzo
1 ½ oz. Bacardi 151 Rum

Shake both ingredients with
ice and strain into a shooter
glass.

Vulcan Death Probe
1 oz. Grain Alcohol
1 oz. White Sambuca

Shake both ingredients with
ice and strain into a shooter
glass.

Vulcan Mind Probe
1 oz. Ouzo
1 oz. Bacardi 151 Rum
1 oz. Wild Turkey 101

Shake all ingredients with ice
and strain into a shooter glass.

VW with the Sunroof Down
1 ½ oz. Vodka
1 oz. Water

Shake both ingredients with
ice and strain into a shooter
glass. Float a lemon slice on
top.

Waffle
1 oz. Butterscotch Schnapps
1 oz. Vodka
1 oz. Orange Juice

Shake all ingredients with ice
and strain into a shooter glass.

War Ace
1 oz. Rum
¼ oz. Blue Curacao
¼ oz. Creme de Noyeaux
1 oz. Pineapple Juice
1 oz. Grape Juice

Shake all ingredients with ice
and strain into a shooter glass.

Warm Carrot Cake
¾ oz. Butterscotch Schnapps
¾ oz. Baileys Irish Cream
¾ oz. Goldschlager

Layer ingredients in order
given in a shooter glass.
Ignite with a match.

Warm Fuzzy Feeling
1 ½ oz. Vodka
½ oz. Sparkling Ribena

Combine both ingredients in a
shooter glass.

Warm Leatherette
1 ½ oz. Black Sambuca
1 oz. Amaretto
¼ oz. Grenadine

Layer ingredients in order
given in a shooter glass.

Water Moccasin
¾ oz. Crown Royal
¾ oz. Peach Schnapps
¾ oz. Lime Juice

Shake all ingredients with ice
and strain into a shooter glass.

Watermelon
1 oz. Southern Comfort
1 oz. Vodka
½ oz. Grenadine
1 ½ oz. Pineapple Juice

Shake all ingredients with ice
and strain into a shooter glass.

Watermelon Chill
1 oz. Watermelon Schnapps
1 oz. Vodka
½ oz. Lemonade
½ oz. Pineapple Juice

Shake all ingredients with ice
and strain into a shooter glass.

Watermelon Cooler
1 oz. Watermelon Schnapps
1 oz. Vodka
½ oz. Orange Juice
½ oz. 7-Up

Shake all ingredients with ice
and strain into a shooter glass.

Watermelon Kamikaze
1 oz. Watermelon Schnapps
1 oz. Vodka
1 oz. Sour Mix

Shake all ingredients with ice
and strain into a shooter glass.

Watermelon Lemondrop
1 oz. Watermelon Schnapps
1 oz. Vodka
1 oz. Lemonade

Shake all ingredients with ice
and strain into a shooter glass.

Watermelon Limedrop
1 oz. Watermelon Schnapps
1 oz. Vodka
1 oz. Limeade

Shake all ingredients with ice
and strain into a shooter glass.

Way Cool
1 oz. Vodka
1 oz. Blue Curacao
1 oz. Lemonade

Shake all ingredients with ice
and strain into a shooter glass.
Float ½ oz. Wilderberry
Schnapps on top.

Wayne Newton
1 oz. Goldschlager
1 oz. Apple Schnapps

Shake both ingredients with
ice and strain into a shooter
glass.

Week at the Beach
½ oz. Apple Schnapps
½ oz. Peach Schnapps
½ oz. Vodka
½ oz. Orange Juice
½ oz. Cranberry Juice

Shake all ingredients with ice
and strain into a shooter glass.

Welch's Grape Juice
1 oz. Vodka
1 oz. Creme de Cassis
1 oz. Orange Juice
Splash of Cola

Shake all ingredients with ice
and strain into a shooter glass.

Well Water
1 oz. Vodka
1 oz. Lemon Juice

Shake both ingredients with
ice and strain into a sugar-
rimmed shooter glass.

Werewolf
1 ½ oz. Jack Daniel's
1 ½ oz. Drambuie

Shake both ingredients with
ice and strain into a shooter
glass.

West Texas Sunrise
½ oz. Tequila
½ oz. Tabasco Sauce

Combine both ingredients in a
shot glass.

Wet & Wild
1 oz. Licor 43
1 oz. Wilderberry Schnapps
1 oz. Orange Juice

Shake all ingredients with ice
and strain into a shooter glass.

Wet Dream
1 oz. Southern Comfort
1 oz. Malibu Rum
Splash of Cranberry Juice
Splash of Pineapple Juice
Splash of 7-Up

Shake all ingredients with ice
and strain into a green-sugar-
rimmed shooter glass.

Wet Pussy
1 oz. Amaretto
1 oz. Butterscotch Schnapps
½ oz. Cream

Layer ingredients in order
given in a shooter glass.

Whammy
1 oz. Rum
1 oz. Apricot Schnapps
1 oz. Orange Juice
½ oz. Cherry Juice

Shake all ingredients with ice
and strain into a shooter glass.
Top with a splash of cola.

What Crisis?
¾ oz. Melon Liqueur
¾ oz. Peach Schnapps
¾ oz. Cranberry Juice
¾ oz. Orange Juice

Shake all ingredients with ice
and strain into a shooter glass.

Whirly Bird
½ oz. Southern Comfort
½ oz. Chambord
½ oz. Midori Melon Liqueur
½ oz. Absolut Citron Vodka
½ oz. Pineapple Juice

Shake all ingredients with ice
and strain into a shooter glass.

Whiskey Worms
1 oz. Whiskey
1 oz. Scotch
4 Gummy Worms

Combine all ingredients in a
shooter glass.

White America
1 ½ oz. Vodka
1 oz. Tang Orange Powder

Stir both ingredients in a
shooter glass until the powder
dissolves.

White Ass
1 oz. Galliano
1 ½ oz. Cream

Shake both ingredients with
ice and strain into a shooter
glass.

White Bull
1 ½ oz. Tequila
½ oz. Kahlua

Shake both ingredients with
ice and strain into a shooter
glass. Float ½ oz. cream on
top.

White House
1 oz. Kahlua
1 oz. Rumple Minze
¼ oz. Bacardi 151 Rum

Layer ingredients in order
given in a shooter glass.
Ignite with a match.

White Lightning
1/3 oz. Vodka
1/3 oz. Tequila
1/3 oz. Gin

Layer ingredients in order
given in a shot glass.

White Spider
1 oz. Vodka
1 oz. White Creme de Menthe

Stir both ingredients with ice
and strain into a shooter glass.

White Wolf
¾ oz. Kahlua
¾ oz. White Sambuca
¾ oz. Baileys Irish Cream

Layer ingredients in order
given in a shooter glass.

Whitman Sampler
1 oz. Light Creme de Cacao
1 oz. Raspberry Liqueur
1 oz. Cream

Shake all ingredients with ice
and strain into a shooter glass.

Whoop Ass
1 oz. Southern Comfort
½ oz. Amaretto
½ oz. Bacardi 151 Rum

Combine all ingredients in a
shooter glass. Ignite with a
match.

Who's Your Daddy
½ oz. Everclear
½ oz. After Shock Cinnamon
Liqueur
½ oz. Cranberry Juice
½ oz. Cherry Kool-Aid

Shake all ingredients with ice
and strain into a shooter glass.

**Why Don't We Get Drunk
& Screw**
1 oz. Cherry Brandy
1 oz. Bacardi 151 Rum
1 oz. Orange Juice
1 oz. Ginger Ale

Shake all ingredients with ice
and strain into a shooter glass.

Why Not
1 oz. Gin
1 oz. Apricot Brandy
½ oz. Dry Vermouth
Dash of Lemon Juice

Shake all ingredients with ice
and strain into a shooter glass.

Wide Glide
½ oz. Peach Schnapps
½ oz. Bacardi Black Rum

Layer ingredients in order
given in a shot glass.

Wild Ass Indian
¾ oz. Smirnoff Vodka
¾ oz. Johnny Walker Red
¾ oz. Bacardi Select Rum

Combine all ingredients in a
shooter glass.

Wild Fuck
1 oz. Wilderberry Schnapps
1 oz. Vodka
1 oz. Orange Juice

Shake all ingredients with ice
and strain into a shooter glass.

Wild Sue
1 ½ oz. Peppermint Schnapps
1 ½ oz. Hawaiian Punch

Shake both ingredients with
ice and strain into a shooter
glass. Float a teaspoonful of
Red Hots candies on top.

Wild Thing
2 oz. Wilderberry Schnapps
1 oz. Orange Juice

Shake both ingredients with
ice and strain into a shooter
glass. Top with a splash of
club soda.

Wild Ward
1 oz. Wilderberry Schnapps
1 oz. Blue Curacao
1 oz. Baileys Irish Cream

Shake all ingredients with ice
and strain into a shooter glass.

Windex
1 ½ oz. Vodka
¾ oz. Triple Sec
¾ oz. Blue Curacao

Shake all ingredients with ice
and strain into a shooter glass.

Windjammer
1 oz. Key Largo Schnapps
1 oz. Cranberry Juice
1 oz. Pineapple Juice

Shake all ingredients with ice
and strain into a shooter glass.

Windshield Washer Fluid
1 ½ oz. Absolut Vodka
½ oz. Blue Curacao

Shake both ingredients with
ice and strain into a shooter
glass.

Windy
¾ oz. Vodka
¾ oz. Blue Curacao
¾ oz. Pineapple Juice
¾ oz. Sour Mix

Shake all ingredients with ice
and strain into a shooter glass.

Wishbone
1 ½ oz. Warm Cognac
1 oz. Warm Maple Syrup

Combine both ingredients in a
shooter glass.

Wolf Pussy
¾ oz. Jack Daniel's
¾ oz. Cuervo Gold Tequila
¾ oz. Rumple Minze

Shake all ingredients with ice
and strain into a shooter glass.

Wolfgang's Revenge
¾ oz. Bacardi 151 Rum
¼ oz. Vodka
¼ oz. Southern Comfort
¼ oz. Jack Daniel's
¼ oz. Grand Marnier
¼ oz. Drambuie
¼ oz. Amaretto

Shake all ingredients with ice
and strain into a shooter glass.

Wolfman Special
1 oz. Kahlua
½ oz. Grand Marnier
½ oz. Baileys Irish Cream
½ oz. Bacardi 151 Rum
½ oz. Amaretto

Shake all ingredients with ice
and strain into a shooter glass.

Woman's Revenge
½ oz. Kahlua
½ oz. Lime Juice

Layer ingredients in order
given in a shot glass.

Wookie
1 ½ oz. Southern Comfort
1 ½ oz. Orange Juice
Pinch of Celery Salt

Shake all ingredients with ice
and strain into a shooter glass.

Woo-Woo
1 oz. Peach Schnapps
1 oz. Vodka
1 oz. Cranberry Juice

Shake all ingredients with ice
and strain into a shooter glass.

Wretched Semen
1 oz. Tequila
1 oz. Light Creme de Cacao
1 oz. Cream

Shake all ingredients with ice
and strain into a shooter glass.
Top with a dash of Grenadine
and a bit of finely chopped
butter.

**Wrigley's Doublemint
Blowjob**
1 oz. Kahlua
½ oz. Peppermint Schnapps
1 ½ oz. Cream

Shake all ingredients with ice
and strain into a shooter glass.

Wrinkled Pecker
1 oz. Rumple Minze
1 oz. Sour Apple Pucker
Schnapps

Shake both ingredients with
ice and strain into a shooter
glass.

X-File
¾ oz. Cognac
¾ oz. Scotch
½ oz. Vodka
½ oz. Gin

Shake all ingredients with ice
and strain into a shooter glass.

XXX Porn Star
1 oz. Peach Schnapps
1 ½ oz. Malibu Rum

Combine both ingredients in a
shooter glass. Top with 5
drops of cream.

Y2K
1 oz. Dark Creme de Cacao
1 oz. Blue Curacao

Layer ingredients in order
given in a shooter glass.

Yak Milk
½ oz. Captain Morgan Parrot
Bay Rum
½ oz. Baileys Irish Cream
½ oz. Light Creme de Cacao

Shake all ingredients with ice
and strain into a shooter glass.

Yankee Panky
¾ oz. Southern Comfort
¾ oz. Amaretto
¾ oz. Malibu Rum
¾ oz. Pineapple Juice

Shake all ingredients with ice
and strain into a shooter glass.

Yeah Dude
1 oz. Grain Alcohol
1 oz. Southern Comfort
1 ½ oz. Cola
Dash of Green Tabasco Sauce

Shake all ingredients with ice
and strain into a shooter glass.

Yellow Bird
1 oz. Rum
1 oz. Creme de Banana
1 oz. Orange Juice

Shake all ingredients with ice
and strain into a shooter glass.

Yellow Fingers
1 oz. Gin
1 oz. Blackberry Brandy
½ oz. Creme de Banana
½ oz. Cream

Shake all ingredients with ice
and strain into a shooter glass.

Yellow Jacket
1 oz. Amaretto di Saronno
1 oz. Tequila
2 oz. Orange Juice

Shake all ingredients with ice
and strain into a shooter glass.

Yellow Nutter
1 oz. Bacardi Limon Rum
1 oz. Sour Mix
1 oz. Citra Soda

Shake all ingredients with ice
and strain into a shooter glass.
Drop a teaspoonful of sugar
into the center of the drink.

Yellow Snow
1 oz. Light Creme de Cacao
1 oz. Pernod
1 oz. Cream

Shake all ingredients with ice
and strain into a shooter glass.

Yikes & Away
1 oz. Jägermeister
1 oz. Bacardi 151 Rum

Layer ingredients in order
given in a shooter glass.

Ying Yang
1 ½ oz. Jägermeister
1 ½ oz. Rumple Minze

Layer ingredients in order
given in a shooter glass.

You Drivea Me Crazy
½ oz. Bacardi 151 Rum
½ oz. Malibu Rum
¼ oz. Pineapple Juice

Combine all ingredients in a
shooter glass. Top with a dash
of Grenadine.

Yukon Torpedo
1 oz. Yukon Jack
1 oz. Ice 101 Peppermint
Schnapps
½ oz. Jack Daniel's
Dash of Lime Juice

Shake all ingredients with ice
and strain into a shooter glass.

Z Street Slammer
1 ¼ oz. Light Rum
¾ oz. Creme de Banana
¾ oz. Pineapple Juice
¼ oz. Grenadine

Shake all ingredients with ice
and strain into a shooter glass.

Zebra
1 ½ oz. Black Sambuca
1 oz. White Tequila

Layer ingredients in order
given in a shooter glass.
Ignite with a match.

Zero Mist
2 oz. White Creme de Menthe
1 oz. Water

Combine both ingredients in a
shooter glass. Chill in the
freezer for at least 2 hours.
Stir until slushy.

Zipper
1 oz. Baileys Irish Cream
1 oz. Grand Marnier
1 oz. Anisette

Shake all ingredients with ice
and strain into a shooter glass.

Zipper Dropper
1 oz. Kahlua
1 oz. Light Creme de Cacao
1 oz. Green Creme de Menthe

Shake all ingredients with ice
and strain into a shooter glass.

Zipperhead
1 oz. Vodka
1 oz. Chambord

Shake both ingredients with
ice and strain into a shooter
glass. Top with a splash of
club soda.

Zombie
1 oz. Light Rum
1 oz. Apricot Schnapps
½ oz. Orange Juice
½ oz. Pineapple Juice

Shake all ingredients with ice
and strain into a shooter glass.

Zombie Crunch
1 oz. Tequila
1 oz. Butterscotch Schnapps
1 oz. Orange Juice

Shake all ingredients with ice
and strain into a shooter glass.

Zombie's Eyeball
¾ oz. Vodka
¾ oz. Tequila
¾ oz. Cold Coffee

Shake all ingredients with ice
and strain into a shooter glass.
Serve with a wedge of lemon.

Zoot Suit Riot
¾ oz. Southern Comfort
¾ oz. Blackberry Brandy
¾ oz. Apricot Brandy
¾ oz. Cranberry Juice

Shake all ingredients with ice
and strain into a shooter glass.

Zowie
1 oz. Creme de Banana
1 oz. Baileys Irish Cream
1 oz. Malibu Rum

Layer ingredients in order
given in a shooter glass.

NOTES & MY RECIPES

NOTES & MY RECIPES

About the Author

Dennis started his career in the restaurant and nightclub industry when he was just 16. Learning the business from the ground up, Dennis quickly realized what "customer service" meant .

At 18, he took a job as a bartender's assistant at an established restaurant in Baltimore, MD. His first assignment was working with John, a 68 year old man who had spent his entire life as a bartender. John, like Dennis, started bartending when he was in his teens, working at a speak-easy during prohibition .

John mentored Dennis, teaching him that working the bar was an art, and the only way to be successful was to know everything you could about your craft. Dennis learned all of the classic cocktail recipes, including some that hadn't been called for in years. In no time, he began working shifts by himself. However, Dennis still had a lot to learn .

The clientele of the restaurant would frequently request a cocktail that Dennis had never heard of. The few cocktail reference books there behind the bar were of little help. Most had only a couple of hundred recipes and rarely had the one that he was looking for. So Dennis would just ask, "Do you know how to make it?" To his relief, most people did. In order to not be stumped again, he began to write the recipes down on 3x5 index cards, storing them in an alphabetical file box for quick reference. As time progressed, that file box grew rapidly.

Dennis eventually moved on, plying his trade at some of the most popular nightclubs in the country. Each club he worked provided the opportunity to expand his cocktail knowledge. As time went by, his drink file expanded to more than 10,000 recipes. Bartenders from restaurants and clubs all over, hearing about his amazing collection, would call Dennis if they needed a recipe that they couldn't find. This "fame" led Dennis into bartender competitions. He won many, including Jose Cuervo's "Best Margarita Contest" and Baltimore's Best Bartender .

Dennis's skill, experience, and knowledge of the bar industry naturally gave him the opportunity to coach and mentor young bartenders, much like John did for him all those years ago. The recipes and instructions included here are the result of those many years' work .

US $19.95